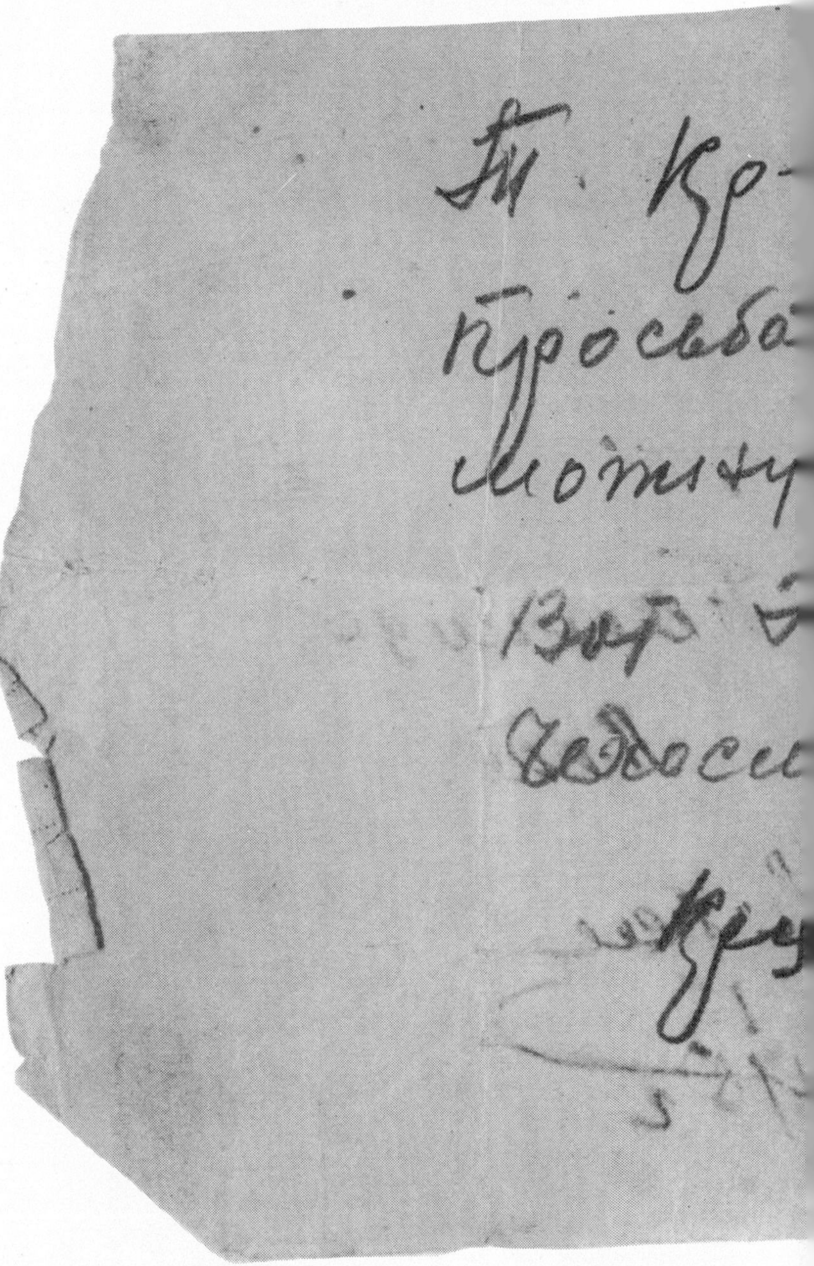

и. командира.

...выводъ все воз-

мощу

Пелангуе

Леве.

...арсен

II
45 г.

# A
# TIME TO SPEAK

# A
# TIME TO SPEAK

·

## Helen Lewis

·

foreword by
**Jennifer Johnston**

THE
BLACKSTAFF
PRESS

———

BELFAST

First published in October 1992 by
The Blackstaff Press Limited
3 Galway Park, Dundonald, Belfast BT16 0AN, Northern Ireland
with the assistance of
The Arts Council of Northern Ireland
Reprinted October 1992

Typeset by Textflow Services Limited

Printed by The Guernsey Press Company Limited

British Library Cataloguing in Publication Data
Lewis, Helen
Time to Speak
I. Title
940.5318092

ISBN 0-85640-491-8

*to Michael, Robin, Daniel, Benjamin,*
*and to the memory of Harry*

to rescue from their separate rooms love and sorrow
*from* 'Ghetto', Michael Longley

It is difficult to categorise this book. I suppose you could say it is an autobiography and leave it at that, yes; but it is slightly other than that. It is an autobiography with the shape and rhythms of a novel, the orderliness of a novel, the heartbeat of a novel. All the baggage of the novelist is here – love and loss, friendship and betrayal, terror and humour, joy and despair, good and evil, death and survival – but there is no fiction, none of the novelist's attention-seeking tricks, nothing is manipulated as a novelist would manipulate, the pattern is inherent not imposed. Helen Lewis does not speculate, she never invents; there is only Truth, witnessed Truth. She tells her story with awesome integrity and in her hands it becomes more than just her story, it becomes history.

This book is the testimony of a woman who has survived the unsurvivable. That in itself is a miracle, if you believe in such things; the book is another. It is written with such stylistic grace that it is impossible to believe that English is not the writer's mother tongue. There is wit and candour as well as sorrow, and a good, controlled anger, which never displays itself in censure or rancour.

Down the years so many people have asked the questions: Why did the Jews allow such things to happen to them? Why did they apparently connive at their own extermination? Helen Lewis addresses these questions: the erosion of civil liberties, the confiscation of bank accounts, the appropriation of flats and houses, the loss of jobs were all astute measures calculated to undermine confidence, to engender anxiety, to alienate the Jewish people from their friends and colleagues. 'Public parks, swimming pools, theatres, cinemas, restaurants and coffee houses were all forbidden to Jews', and Helen's own promising career as a dancer came to an end when she was no longer permitted to perform in any productions. The ration cards issued to Jews were worth much less than those given to everyone else. They had to travel in special carriages in trains and trams and only during certain hours. Their radios were confiscated. Everywhere there were spies – people who seemed only too happy to tell the authorities if their Jewish neighbours stepped out of line, or communicated with non-Jewish friends. The yellow star became the ultimate sign of their isolation: a whole race, people from all walks of life – rich, poor, artists, artisans, shopkeepers, businessmen, teachers – had become pariahs, outcasts from the society in which they had lived and worked. All this was intended to isolate and demoralise them in preparation for deportation.

Deportation to where? For how long? There were only the unacceptable rumours that no one dared to believe. The Jews went into the transports frightened, bewildered people, with nothing – no comfort, little hope, quite unprepared for what had been prepared for them.

It is all too easy to dismiss as monsters the torturers, the humiliators, the murderers, but we must always remember that though there were monsters all right, the majority of these people were ordinary men and women with families of their own. What happened to turn those men and women from the paths of humanity can happen again and it is important that we do not forget, and that we do not allow our children to forget, the terrors we have seen in our lifetime. The suffering of millions in the camps of Hitler and Stalin, in the prisons of Romania, South Africa and Chile, the disappeared, the despairing, the prisoners of conscience and of political expediency must all be remembered, not least because of their suffering, but also to ensure that such things will never be allowed to happen again.

I quote from Ecclesiastes:

> To every thing there is a season, and a time to every purpose under the heaven:
> A time to be born, and a time to die;
> A time to kill, and a time to heal;
> A time to weep, and a time to laugh; a time to mourn, and a time to dance;
> A time to keep silence, and a time to speak.

Helen Lewis has chosen her time to speak.

Only the dead know the whole truth and some of those witnesses who survived have taken upon themselves the painful task of speaking for them. It is our task to listen and never to forget.

JENNIFER JOHNSTON
DERRY, MARCH 1992

# 1

As a young child, my only regret was that I had no little brother or sister to play with and therefore had to find my playmates outside my home. I was, by all accounts, a cheerful, uncomplicated and companionable child; however, occasionally I displayed a resistance to some aspects of bourgeois upbringing that was probably born from an early romantic notion about equality among all peoples.

We lived in Trutnov in a spacious comfortable flat in a big house owned by my family, with my grandparents living in the flat below, an arrangement which made family life slightly claustrophobic at times. As the only child about, I was loved and spoiled by all, but in moments of childish rebellion and loneliness I sought the company of the family cat, Lumpi, or took refuge in the arms of Gusti, the maid, who played an all-important role in my upbringing. Gusti was a patriotic Czech; my family, like the great majority in our small border town in the Sudetenland, was German in language, in culture and in outlook.

I found another division in our society when I started at the local primary school for girls, where I made friends with children from quite different social backgrounds. Before then, I had taken for granted our comfortable well-furnished home with the splendid grand piano and the enormous well-stocked bookcase. To my astonishment and slight unease I found that some of my new friends lived in small, cramped apartments, where, without a 'Gusti', their mothers did all their own housework, while my mother, her share done, dressed up and went out in the afternoons. I was not sure which I preferred, and when I raised the question at home, I was met with amused surprise from my parents and with scorn from Gusti, who disapproved of the awakening of my social conscience.

Both my parents were great music lovers, and my mother was an outstanding pianist as well. Listening to her playing and singing, I became familiar early on with songs by Schubert, Brahms and Schumann. From my gentle, ailing grandfather I learned to love the poetry of Goethe, Schiller and Heine. My father read me Greek and Norse legends and told me exciting stories – the plots of operas – which I then acted out with friends. At the age of six I was sent to my first dance class, and on my return home I announced firmly that I was going to be a dancer. Without anyone realising it, the decision of a lifetime had been made.

Gradually dance became a vital force in my life, as I slowly progressed from my first childish attempts to a more serious pursuit, in which I was guided, sometimes criticised and in the main gently encouraged by my parents. At the age of ten I was even allowed to attend an international dance summer school for children at Laxenburg, near Vienna.

At grammar school I became aware of more serious divisions and subdivisions in our national and religious life. I was Jewish, but less Jewish than some of my friends, whose families observed the Jewish laws and rituals much more strictly than my own. I was also German, but not the same fervently nationalistic type of German as some of my classmates. My home was the democratic Republic of Czechoslovakia; my mother tongue was German, my religion was Jewish. When did I wonder for the first time where I really belonged? For a while I became an enthusiastic member of a Zionist youth movement, but only for a while: my family leaned heavily against any form of exclusiveness.

At school I formed friendly and uncomplicated relationships with teachers and fellow pupils until about 1933, when the first reverberations of events from across the border reached the German communities in Czechoslovakia, and permeated every sphere of life, even the classroom. From now on, innocence and trust were put to the test. At home there was endless talk of the new, horrifying developments in Germany, and the first refugees appeared among us.

There was an incident at school in my German literature class. A girl – a close friend of mine – gave a talk about Frederick the Great, which was a scarcely concealed eulogy of Hitler. The class received it with delight. Somehow, word of this reached the Czech authorities, who reacted with alarm and set up an inquiry. The girl, who by now had become a nationalist heroine, and was soon to be a martyr, was reprimanded, and the class reacted by proclaiming a boycott of its three Jewish pupils, one of whom was wrongly assumed to have been the source of the leak. It was a sad and chilling experience, which raised in my mind the first serious questions about friendship and loyalty.

In the summer holidays of that year, 1934, my father died tragically and unexpectedly. Overnight, the sheltered, warm security of my home collapsed, and afterwards nothing was ever the same again.

My last year at school was geared towards the final exams, which were all-important and could determine our future. All other considerations slipped into the background, and we were once again classmates, if not friends. I passed with very good results and it was expected that I would go to university to study languages or literature, which had been my best subjects. My family and their friends and many of my teachers were aghast when I decided instead to study dance as a professional career. My mother, with faith in my sincerity and hope in my talent, supported me in every way, and so, at the end of the holidays, she and I said goodbye to our home, family, and friends and moved into a small flat in Prague to start a new life.

Prague was a revelation. On my previous brief visits I had seen and admired the famous historical sites and the city's architectural beauty. Now, with astonishment and delight, I came to discover the richness and variety of Czech cultural life. My immediate and most obvious introduction was through my dance school.

After a full week of auditioning for a place, I received a letter that stated that while I was totally lacking in experience, I had sufficient talent to be accepted for three years' professional training. I was jubilant, but shaken all the same by the realisation that years of acclaim as a dancer in my little home town had left me an absolute beginner.

Alongside my hard and often gruelling training, I was initiated into Czech music, art and literature, things which until then had been missing from my education. My rudimentary knowledge of the Czech language improved rapidly, and fellow students soon became friends. I was in great awe of Milča Mayerová, the director of the dance school, who was also its principal teacher. She was a quite superb choreographer and teacher, but not always a sensitive or patient educator. There were many occasions when in secret I cried from frustration at the slowness of my progress, but I invariably took care to present a cheerful façade to my mother, who had helped me to realise my dream and was paying for it out of her own pocket.

I was still under pressure from the family and my former teachers to study something more 'practical' than dance; eventually I gave in and enrolled at the German University in Prague to study philosophy. The choice of subject was determined by my sense of priorities: the philosophy curriculum would interfere least with my dance timetable.

On Sundays I often explored Prague and the countryside in the company of my mother, and in the evenings I went to as many concerts, operas and plays as I had time for and could afford. At the end of that first difficult year of studying dance, I had a morale-lifting success: there was a choreography competition for the entire school, and I won the top prize.

Holidays were spent in Trutnov, swimming and walking in the mountains; but it was not home any longer. I had changed and grown away from many of my former friends, and they, in turn, had developed interests that were very different from mine. I saw a great deal of my friend Harry at that time, but he too seemed bewildered at my single-minded devotion to my chosen career.

When I returned to school it became clear to my teachers and colleagues, as well as to myself, that a dramatic change had taken place. I had absorbed and assimilated the first year's teaching during the weeks of holiday and rest, and now I found myself on the same level as the other students and making rapid progress. In no time at all I was even given small parts in the school's professional dance company. Nineteen thirty-seven was my miraculous year: I resumed private studies of French and passed a major examination in French language and literature, as well as my philosophy preliminaries at the university.

One day in a philosophy class I became uncomfortably aware of a young man sitting next to me, who was eyeing me with extraordinary interest, and it came as no surprise when at the end of the lecture he pressed a crumpled piece of paper into my hand. It was a vicious Nazi propaganda leaflet. For whatever reason, I must have been deemed to be a suitable recruit to their cause. I was deeply shocked and dismayed and felt that my eyes had been opened to an outside world I had preferred to ignore. I did not know what to do, and in the end, just like so many others, I did nothing.

Towards the end of my second year at dance school, teaching practice was introduced into the syllabus. Right from the start I found it fascinating, much to the surprise of most of the other students, who considered it a time-consuming nuisance. I pursued this new activity, and as I grew in confidence I was given a few of the school's amateur classes to teach. With learning, teaching and rehearsing, my life was full, time was short, and all my interests were bound up with my art. Whenever Harry and I met we both realised that we were steadily growing apart, and after one particularly stormy meeting, he decided that he was tired of competing with dance for my attention, and so we parted.

One evening a friend introduced me to a young man, who, to our mutual surprise, turned out to live in the same apartment block as my mother and I. The three of us decided to go to a beauty spot in the countryside near Prague the following Sunday, but at the last moment our friend could not join us and Paul and I went alone on a long walk, which, unknown to us, was to lead to an entirely new destination.

During the holidays, I took a job at a children's summer

camp near Prague, looking after the children all day, as well as teaching gymnastics and dance and coaching them in swimming. It was hard work and I was paid really no more than pocket money, but the experience confirmed that my interest in teaching was no mere whim.

I had one more year to study. At the start of the year I passed my final French exam, and while celebrating the happy occasion, Paul and I considered for the first time the possibility of a common future. In the late spring of 1938 I successfully completed my studies at the dance school and obtained my diploma. I was now fully qualified as a dancer–choreographer–teacher. I quietly dropped the idea of taking a degree at the German University. In that year it looked very doubtful if I would ever reap any benefit from it. Germany's expansionism increasingly posed a threat to Czechoslovakia, and in response, on 21 May, the first Czech mobilisation took place, and was then rescinded. In June Paul and I were married.

We spent the first and last carefree weeks of our married life on a beautiful, romantic island in Yugoslavia, and then set up home in a Prague full of uncertainty and foreboding. I became a housewife, in name at least, but without the slight-est idea of what that involved. Luckily my mother had found us Pepička, who ran the household efficiently but who some-times did not conceal her disdain for my obvious shortcom-ings. If I offered some timid opinion on a domestic question, she always responded, 'You, Madame, you go dancing', and this I gladly and gratefully did.

I assisted in the running of the school, I danced in the company, and I even taught a few private pupils of my own.

We were happy, even though we knew that our country, and with it our freedom and democracy, were in extreme danger. And so we lived through the autumn mobilisation, the Munich crisis, the humiliating demobilisation of the Czech army, and ultimately the destruction of our republic. President Beneš left the country, and his successor, President Hácha, established the so-called 'Second Republic'. There was an immediate influx of refugees from the Sudetenland, which had been annexed by Germany, among them my Uncle Erwin, and Paul's sister Julie and her family. It was a mercy that my grandmother, now widowed, had died the previous year in her own home and so had been spared the indignity and heartbreak of enforced emigration.

One day, when visiting an old friend, I met Harry again. As an unregistered refugee from the Sudetenland, homeless and jobless, he was living a precarious and half-illegal existence in Prague. We were glad to see each other, and I invited him to our home. It was an evening both of happy reminiscences and of gloomy speculation about the future.

Everywhere the conversation was about emigration, and Paul sounded out the possibilities of a job in Australia, which ended in disappointment.

In November the National Theatre invited our dance company to take part in a prestigious production of Molière's *Le Malade Imaginaire*. The many famous names in the cast included the celebrated Olga Scheinpflugová, wife of the writer Karel Čapek. To dance on the stage of that great theatre was an act of love and for a time the outside realities faded. Milča Mayerová danced the principal role in the major dance interlude between two acts of the play. After a few performances

9

she decided that I should take over from her, and started to rehearse me in the part. Then, suddenly, it was all over. Karel Čapek died, and all performances were cancelled as a mark of respect and grief. The nation was stunned. Karel Čapek had represented all that was best in the great democratic and humanistic tradition of Tomáš Masaryk's First Republic. His death at that moment – Christmas 1938 – marked the end of an era. We now entered the new year: 1939.

## 3

On 15 March 1939 I had tonsillitis. I had not been ill for years, but the attack was severe enough for my mother to come to our flat to nurse me. I fretted badly. Milča Mayerová had started work on Milhaud's *La Création du Monde*, in which I was to dance the principal part, and now I was missing rehearsals.

On the previous evening there had been ominous news on the radio. Apparently there were German troop movements in the border areas, and there was talk of general unrest. We thought it would be wise for my mother to spend the night at our home, to avoid travelling to her flat on the other side of Prague. Together we listened to the radio news again early next morning. President Hácha, we were told, had placed the country in the hands of the Führer for its 'protection' and in consequence there were German tanks and infantry on the streets of Prague. At the end of the broadcast the Czech national anthem was played, for the last time.

As we sat trying to take in this shattering news the telephone rang. It was the caretaker of the block of flats where my mother lived. Mother's niece Herta, and Arnošt her husband, had heard the news and jumped out of the window of their fifth-floor apartment. They were lying dead in the street. Would my mother please come at once and look after Aunt Ida, Herta's mother? Herta and Arnošt had lived in Germany in the early 1930s, just at the time when Hitler came to power. Under the protection of their Czech citizenship they had lived through the early persecutions of the German Jews and had been deeply affected by what they had witnessed. Arnošt was a Czech patriot and a Jew, and that morning's news was the end of their world. I remember very little of what followed. The shock, coming on top of my illness, left me too weak even to go to their funeral.

In the next weeks we lived through waves of despair and hope, frantic activity and paralysing apathy. We talked and debated interminably, and endlessly asked ourselves the same questions. Was it really true and irrevocable that the republic had ceased to exist and had become a 'Protectorate'? Who was protecting whom, and from what? Had Hitler really waved from the very window in Hradčany Castle where once stood Masaryk, the embodiment of the highest humanist ideals?

Many people who had been prominent in Czech cultural and political life had already been arrested, and everyone thought and spoke of emigration. Paul and I were no exception, but whenever we seriously considered it, we had to face the fact that we would have to leave behind his parents and my mother. Neither of us could even contemplate this possibility. So we did nothing – we stayed. Life began to return to a kind of normality, or so it seemed for a time. Some of our friends left the country. Until the end of March it was possible to get into England, but after that, the authorities there only allowed in people with entry visas, and visas were difficult to obtain. On one of the last days of March I met Harry by chance in Wenceslas Square. 'I am so glad to see you once more,' he said. 'I am leaving for London tonight.' We shook hands and wished each other luck.

Friends who had emigrated could still write to us. Their first letters were far from cheerful. They were lonely, they were penniless, and they felt unwanted. Many found it very difficult to adjust and some of them almost seemed to regret that they had left.

We, too, had adjustments to make. Jobs were lost and bank accounts frozen. Cultural life became inaccessible. Above all, there was all around us an intangible menace that rendered us first cautious and then fearful in what we said and did. We learned to listen in silence, to read between the lines, to say very little and to trust nobody. Paul had particular difficulties at work. The owner of the glove factory which he managed was in London, where she cashed in her foreign accounts, regardless of the consequences for those of us at home. Paul was threatened by the *Devisenschutzsonderkommando*, the special economic task force of the SS. One day they came and rifled our flat in search of a suspected hoard of foreign currency. They of course found nothing, but ours was one of the first bank accounts to be confiscated.

I still went to Milča Mayerová for classes, and I still taught at her school, but I had to resign myself to the fact that in future I would not be allowed to take part in any major productions. I had just reached the stage in my career where, after so many years of working and hoping, I was to dance important roles. It was bitter to accept that this would not now happen. As it was, I still appeared in a few performances, but under an assumed name, in a little studio theatre, or at the occasional matinée.

13

One day a young man presented himself to Paul and asked urgently to be given a job, any job, in the glove factory. He had been an officer in the Czech army. Now the Government was setting up a puppet regiment of Czech soldiers who were to serve the new order. He could not bear the thought of joining, but if he was not to be conscripted, he had to have a job. He had no qualifications to speak of, but Paul took to him immediately and, at some risk to himself, gave him a job. In this strange way we came to know Danny, who was to become one of our dearest and most faithful friends.

New anti-Jewish laws were promulgated in early summer: public parks, swimming pools, theatres, cinemas, restaurants and coffee houses were all forbidden to Jews and had to display an appropriate sign. Surprisingly we were still able to travel on buses and trains, and we spent most weekends at Dobříš, a place we came to love dearly. There we had good friends, Jews and non-Jews; the little town was picturesque and charming, with a big lake for happy, unrestricted swimming. In the summer of 1939 Prague was oppressive and full of menace, but on the bus to Dobříš we began to relax, and once we arrived, we could for at least a few hours forget that we lived on the brink.

When we met Erwin in 1939, he was a good-looking, well-mannered young man in his late teens. He was Jewish and lived with his elderly parents in the same apartment block as Paul and myself. They had previously lived in the Sudetenland, their Czech was poor and they gave the impression of being lonely and lost in the capital.

Erwin certainly had no friends, nor did he have a job or even an occupation. We used to meet him in the lift and when we noticed that he appeared eager to talk to us, we invited him in a few times for a cup of coffee and a chat. On these occasions he spoke sadly of his difficulties in communicating with his parents, his longing for young company and, most frequently and vehemently, of his hopeless, black view of the future – his own, ours, everybody's. He could be charming, but every so often the negative side of his personality emerged in a way that was disturbing in a young man, even at that time. One thing was clear – he enjoyed these visits and was grateful for the occasional invitation, and we, feeling rather sorry for him, did our best to make him feel welcome.

More and more of our friends left, once they had secured visas and affidavits, and many of those who stayed behind became severely depressed. All the time there were rumours and tales. Sometimes we heard of little acts of kindness, but there were also reminders of the changes that had taken place in the hearts and minds of many.

The summer passed, and with it the Polish crisis and finally the news of an ultimatum. After the betrayal of 'peace in our time' at Munich the previous year, we were sceptical and had little faith in our former allies. The British declaration of war therefore took us by surprise. We were overjoyed. Now our German masters would feel the onslaught of the mighty allied forces; now they would need all their power and cunning to defend themselves, and they would turn their attention away from us. Perhaps they could hold out until Christmas, by then it would all be over.

We set off to celebrate with our friends in Dobříš, but when we returned to Prague, we found Paul's parents desolate. Paul's sister Julie, along with her little son Peter, had been forced on to the last train to London by her father-in-law, and she was on her way there now, where her husband was already waiting for her. She and Paul had been very close, I myself had loved her as if she were my own sister and we hadn't been able to say goodbye. It was a measure of our ignorance of things to come that we considered this episode a tragedy.

Germany was not defeated overnight as we had hoped, and the Jews' position went into a serious deterioration in every respect. Food rationing was introduced and cards distributed, but the Jews' cards were worth much less than those issued to everyone else and shopping was allowed only between three and five in the afternoon, when the shelves were mostly empty. We could still take the trams, but had to travel in the second or third carriage, and then only at certain hours. We were under curfew from eight in the evening until seven the following morning. My mother was evicted from her flat in Prague 7, a district favoured by Germans. She was fortunate to find another very small flat in Branik, fairly close to where Paul and I lived.

On a spring day in 1940 Paul and I were informed that thanks to Julie's efforts in London we had been issued with entry visas for Shanghai. Our ship would leave from Trieste in ten days. We just looked at each other sadly, each knowing what the other felt. There were no circumstances now in which we would abandon our parents. In 1939, when so many people fled, they could do so fondly imagining that their relatives would soon follow. But by 1940 we were under no such illusion, and all we could see was the unbearable loneliness and helplessness of those left behind. All the same, to give ourselves just a little more time to think, we sent a telegram to the shipping company in Trieste, and asked to be transferred to the next ship, which was due to leave two weeks later. A few days afterwards, Italy joined the war, and with immense relief, we gave up the idea of our rescue.

We continued to go to Dobříš from time to time, but with the increasingly uneasy feeling that we were being watched. We happened to be there in June 1940 when the news came through of the fall of France. On that day we buried our last hope.

## 4

By 1941 the daily onslaught of vicious anti-Semitism from the newspapers and radio had prepared the ground for a new anti-Jewish law that made all previous ones look like harmless games: the introduction of the yellow star, to be worn in public at all times by all Jews over the age of six. From that moment we were visible targets for anyone who chose to abuse or attack us and the psychological effects were cleverly and cruelly calculated to impress upon us that we were outcasts who had no place in society.

In the streets of Prague we became painfully aware of the stares of passers-by, some embarrassed, some openly hostile, some even surprised if one did not seem to look Jewish. The averted eye was often as hurtful as the open sneer; a quick glance of sympathy gave little comfort when accompanied by a hasty step sideways. The knowledge that we were marked out gave rise to bewildering, conflicting feelings. Was the star a sign of distinction or of humiliation or did this depend on the wearer? Had our humanity and dignity been taken away from us along with all our other rights? Was it an act of defiance or cowardice to go out without wearing it? Some people did not leave their homes any longer; others tried to be philosophical; a few committed suicide. A young couple in our house had a peculiar problem. Their five-year-old son cried bitterly because he wanted a lovely yellow star like Mummy's and Daddy's to show the other children when he played with them in the street – which in any case he was not supposed to do.

Our isolation was, in theory, now complete. To maintain contact with non-Jewish friends was to expose them to immense danger. Friendship with Jews was by definition an act of treachery towards the Reich and denunciation was a patriotic deed, which kept busy all those who now made a career of spying on their fellow citizens. Nevertheless, none of our Czech friends took the slightest notice, and we kept up our relationships as before, sometimes right under the noses of spies and collaborators.

Paul lost his job and was replaced by a commissar appointed by the German government. A well-known lawyer, who before the war had represented Paul's company, offered him work in his office. A courageous gesture like this lifted our morale and helped us fight the depression that engulfed so many others. My friends from dancing days still called to see me. We even made some new friends. Adolf was a big, gentle man who lived in a flat three floors above ours. We had met in the lift and exchanged a few words as we sized each other up. Our careful, hesitant invitation was eagerly accepted, and we became friends. Adolf was single and an electrical engineer. He was intelligent, sensitive and generous, and possessed a marvellous sense of humour: we laughed more in his company than at any other time. We shared a love of music and played records to each other in his flat or ours: Bach's Fourth Brandenburg Concerto, Beethoven's Archduke Trio, the Brahms Double Concerto, Suk's *Radůz and Mahulena*, and many others, but most often, Dvořák's Cello Concerto. We also shared the services of

Pepička, our cleaning lady, who seemed so devoted to all of us.

After we had been ordered to hand in our radios to the authorities, the pattern of our meetings with Adolf changed. At a certain hour in the night, Paul and I tiptoed quietly upstairs. Huddled together in front of that little instrument of hope, we listened to the voice of Jan Masaryk, the Czech foreign minister exiled in London, while our eyes avoided the printed label on the radio that proclaimed that 'listening to the enemy is punishable by death'. There were Czech Fascists and Germans living in the building, and we all knew that these hours together were dangerous.

I sometimes took risks of my own. Milča Mayerová gave the premières of new works in the Vinohrady Theatre. I could not stay away and slipped in to see a matinée without telling anyone. Brokenhearted, I watched a programme that included some of Smetana's *Czech Dances*, and Dvořák's *Golden Spinning Wheel*. Milča Mayerová even told me which parts would have been mine to perform. Many years later I exorcised the pain of that memory when I choreographed and performed those works with my own dance group in Belfast.

I visited my mother, sometimes outside the permitted hours. She found her new flat very lonely. None of her friends lived nearby and she was only happy when we were together. Of course, she worried when I turned up unexpectedly at her door, my star hidden behind a big handbag clutched to my chest; but I always managed to make light of it while I was with her. Then her door would close behind me and I had to face the hostile streets on my way home to my desperately worried husband.

One morning, before the hours when Jews were allowed to go shopping, I came out of a music shop, where I had bought a recording of *Le Carnaval Romain* by Berlioz as a birthday present for Paul, and ran straight into an old school friend from Trutnov. I was of course not wearing the star. He was overjoyed to see me. I pretended the same. We talked for a few minutes, saying very little, avoiding any sensitive question. I was anxious to go home; he offered to accompany me. But if he took me home, he would find out where I lived and he could denounce me. Was he the type? I did not know, and I could scarcely ask. Nor could I find an excuse to stop him from seeing me home. So we walked together back to my flat, and afterwards, for a few days, I waited for the ring at the door. I need not have worried. When we met again in Trutnov after the war he told me his story. He was a doctor, and during the deportations of Jews he had issued false certificates to his patients to save them, at least for a time. His reward, after the liberation, was to be exempted from the expulsions of Sudeten Germans to Germany.

There were sometimes grotesque, almost farcical, incidents. One evening our friend Franta felt that he had to come and see us, despite the curfew and his striking Jewish appearance. He discarded his star and took a crowded tram to our flat. A very drunken man was shouting obscenities about the Nazis at the top of his voice, all across the carriage. There was no reaction: everyone was afraid and pretended not to hear. Frustrated, the drunk turned to Franta, and shouted out even louder, 'You there, you're a Jew, surely you agree that they're the world's biggest bastards.' Franta froze in horror, but everyone else broke into uncontrollable laughter.

It was his good luck there was no collaborator on the tram, but when he arrived at our flat he was near to collapse, and he had to stay the night.

Now and then Paul and I went in the afternoon to chamber music concerts at the home of Jewish friends. There I met Hilde, who was also from Trutnov. She told me her husband now lived in a distant place called Belfast, in Ireland. The outbreak of war had prevented her from joining him there, but occasionally, very occasionally, she heard from him via Switzerland. I learned from her that Harry had also found a haven in that same place. When I mentioned this to my mother, she reminded me with bitter tears that I could be safe out there if I had married him, instead of allowing dance to break up our romance. Shortly afterwards, the papers were full of reports of devastating air raids on Belfast, with thousands of casualties. My mother said sadly, 'Nowhere is safe any more', and after that we did not speak of Harry again.

# 5

As soon as the Protectorate was established in March 1939 every Jew had to register with the Central Jewish Office, which had been set up by command of the German authorities to deal with Jewish affairs. In the autumn of 1941, when the first orders for deportations were issued, these same registers formed the basis for swift and efficient implementation. Within a matter of a few days a transport of two thousand people was summoned, assembled, and dispatched. Those who received the summons had to leave behind their homes and their belongings in immaculate condition. The flats and their contents were confiscated by the German authorities, who then passed them on to new owners of their own choosing. Each deportee was permitted to take fifty kilos of luggage, the only worldly goods they were to possess.

And so, these distraught, bewildered people had to choose what would be indispensable for their future life. Not knowing what this future was going to be, it was a harrowing task to make any choice. Which imperishable food to take, and how much? What clothing, and for how long, and for what conditions? Was there any need of bedclothes and blankets? Was there room for them? How could you find space for a little cooker? Of course, one needed washing and toilet articles to keep up standards of cleanliness and hygiene. There must be a few medicines for all eventualities. Was it selfish and irresponsible to take a cherished book and a few family photographs? In their frantic efforts to make the right choices, people used up their precious physical and emotional energies and arrived spent and exhausted at the Trade Fair Hall, which had been turned into the official assembly point.

The first transports went east to Łódź, in Poland, where the deportees disappeared into a huge ghetto. We knew nothing at home, not even where they had gone to, until after a few weeks their carefully worded postcards began to arrive. A young married couple we had been friendly with had been in the first transport; the postcard we received said our friend was a widow.

Shortly afterwards, two transports, made up entirely of young men, were sent to a little garrison town north of Prague which had been evacuated. They were to set up and prepare our own ghetto, one that was to house – or was it to concentrate? – the whole Jewish population of Bohemia and Moravia, as well as some Jews, mainly the elderly, from Germany, Austria, Denmark and the Netherlands. This was the birth of the ghetto at Theresienstadt, which the Czechs knew as Terezín, and from then on it was only a question of time before each of us had to pack and leave home.

Summons followed summons, and transport followed transport. Erwin and his parents said goodbye and were not heard of again. Almost every day you could see people of all ages making their way to the assembly point, dragging their luggage through the streets and on to the trams. Any offer of help was inadvisable, even any sign of sympathy could be dangerous. People looked away in embarrassment and shame.

Not all of them did so. One evening Danny and his young wife Růžena paid us one of their most welcome visits. As soon as the door had closed behind them Danny took off his overcoat and stood there in front of us in the full splendour of his uniform as a captain of the Czech army, every button freshly polished. 'Just to remind you of our past and give you some hope for the future,' he said and saluted smartly. It may sound like a childish gesture now, but at the time, it gave our crushed spirits an enormous uplift.

One Sunday morning I was woken by an unbearable toothache. My face was badly swollen and I felt feverish. I rang the dentist, who agreed to see me at once. It was a bitterly cold day and I reached for my winter coat. In the hurry, plagued by pain, I tore the yellow star off my raincoat, and disregarding the strict rule that it should be sewn firmly into place, I stuck it on to my winter coat with pins, one pin at each corner of the star, and rushed away. The dentist lanced and drained the abscess, gave me an injection, and sent me home with the advice that I should go to bed. I left the surgery, still dazed by pain and shock, and made my way back to the tram. Suddenly I was stopped by a huge Czech policeman, his accusing finger pointing at my coat. Looking down, I immediately understood the enormity of the offence I was committing. The star was dangling down, precariously held in place by only two of the pins. The others had fallen out on the way. 'You come with me,' he thundered, and I was under arrest. Within a few minutes I was in the nearest police station.

There, he let me know his intentions and my destiny. He would immediately prepare a report which would include all personal information about me and a detailed description of the criminal act I had committed. He would then submit this report to his German superiors. In view of the gravity of the case, they would undoubtedly send me at once to the assembly point for inclusion in the transport waiting there to depart. I would most certainly not be allowed to communicate with my family. The other policemen in the room stared at their desks in silence. While he was still enjoying his moment of glory, a telephone rang in another room, and he was called away. 'You wait here,' he ordered and was gone.

As soon as the door had closed behind him the other policemen sprang into action. One watched the window for his return, and another brought me a cup of tea. Most important, a third brought needle and thread.

'Sew the damned thing on as fast as you can, then run before he gets back,' he said.

'What will you tell him?' I asked, sewing for my life.

They looked at one another, then one said, 'Leave that to us, you just hurry up.'

I finished my sewing, and thanking them from the bottom of my heart, I left and ran all the way home.

On the last day of 1941 our little family gathered in our flat to see in the new year, and to be together one more time. We tried desperately to be cheerful and good-humoured, knowing very well that we were not deceiving each other. Each of us – Paul's parents, my mother, Paul and I – had contributed to a good meal, and now we talked of the past, avoiding any allusion to the future, to spare each other the pain and foreboding we felt in our hearts. When eventually we all found space to sleep in the little flat, I did not even dare cry in case they heard me.

Even before 1942 Jews had had to hand over to the German authorities not only their radios but jewellery and silver, furs, and anything of value. What else was there to take from them? Unbelievably, the answer was their pets, those innocent little friends which in many cases were the only joys left in a darkened world. To some, especially children and old people, this was the hardest blow. On the prescribed day, there they were in the trams, white-faced, choking back tears, clutching their pathetic little boxes, cartons or bundles, which were to be handed in at the reception centres: guinea-pigs and hamsters, white mice and tortoises, and of course caged birds. Dogs and cats were the worst, they cried aloud all the way, as if they knew. Paul's father, a tall, calm gentleman, always dignified, had to hand over his much-loved canary, Pepiček. That evening he seemed smaller, shrunken and forlorn.

As more and more Germans moved into the Protectorate, flats owned by Jews became a desirable commodity. The procedure was quick and simple, and conducted with typical efficiency. The interested parties inspected the flats they wanted. If they were suitable, the Jewish owners were evicted as quickly as possible and sent in the next transport to Terezín, where there would be bunk beds waiting for them.

One afternoon our doorbell rang, and outside stood a young German officer with his batman. He saluted politely and presented an official paper, which informed me that the lieutenant had permission to inspect our flat at his convenience. I tried to keep my composure and invited him

27

in. He removed his cap, which in the circumstances I thought an odd gesture, and looking around, he explained in an easy and unselfconscious manner that he had only recently arrived in Prague. He and his wife had temporary accommodation in a guest house, but this flat would be ideal for them. Had we, he wanted to know, made our arrangements for moving out to our new home? When would it suit us to go? In a flash I understood that this lieutenant had no idea at all of the reality of Jewish life in the Protectorate. I looked straight into his eyes and said, 'There is no need to worry about such things, Herr Leutnant, because as soon as you decide to take our flat, we shall be deported in the next transport to Theresienstadt.' For a long time he stood looking at a painting and did not speak. Then he turned abruptly towards me with what I thought was a wink, as if to say, 'I can't speak in *his* presence.' But all he actually said was, 'I shall be back, *auf Wiedersehen*', and putting on his cap, left, the batman following. That evening I told Paul that we would have to start thinking of packing our fifty kilos each.

Nothing happened the next day, but in the evening, when the doorbell rang, Paul and I looked at each other before opening. Outside, there stood a pleasant-looking young couple, smiling shyly, the man clutching a big shopping bag. Out of uniform, I did not recognise him until he said quietly in German, 'Please may we come in?' They introduced themselves formally, then asked, almost timidly, if they could sit down for a while. There were things he wanted to explain, which he could not say in the presence of his batman. They had also taken the liberty of bringing along a few little things we might like, did we mind? From the shopping bag, he brought out fine wine, cigarettes – a luxury to us – and a huge ham. Paul and I, in a daze, acted as hosts to these unlikely guests, and the moment we lifted our glasses to drink each other's health, I felt hysteria rising.

My earlier instinct had been right. Our lieutenant knew hardly anything of the persecution of the Jews in the countries under German occupation. His innocence and the ignorance which was its cause were unbelievable. We listened in silence to his repeated protestations that he would never hurt us or anyone else, that he disagreed with the anti-Jewish laws, that he was an officer of the German army, not a Nazi. He had become very agitated, and his wife looked embarrassed. What on earth were we to do or even to think? He carried on with his tirade about the injustices that were being done every day and his pessimistic view of how the war would end and the retribution that must follow. By the time he had done, he had talked high treason. We had to remind him that the walls in modern houses were thin, and that our neighbours were Germans who might not share his unpatriotic sentiments. Eventually, after a glass or two, we relaxed sufficiently to believe that he meant what he said. Before they finally left, they asked if we would allow them to call again, and when we agreed – what else could we do? – they thanked us warmly for our hospitality. After they had gone, we laughed without humour for a while, before starting to worry about the possible consequences of this bizarre episode.

They did come back, always bringing some delicacies we had forgotten existed, always concerned for our 'well-being'. A few times he was dangerously reckless, not bothering to change out of uniform before he called. These visits were a cause of great tension and worry for us, in case one of our friends or neighbours noticed the caller in German army uniform. How could we explain the inexplicable and who would have believed the unbelievable?

It was at about the same time we noticed a change in Pepička's manner and behaviour. She began to tell us stories she had heard about Jewish families who gave many of their possessions to their home help. And there were other families she knew of who had given nothing, and then when they committed some tiny act of transgression, what did they find but that these trusted ladies denounced them to the authorities. I listened without paying a great deal of attention. Pepička had been with us a long time and I looked upon her as a friend.

We knew, and we resented, that after our inevitable departure, all the lovely things in our flat would end up as cheap loot for the Gestapo. Adolf and Danny came to the rescue, well aware of the grave risks to themselves of saving and hiding Jewish property. In the still of the night, glass, porcelain, books and records made their way upstairs to Adolf's impeccably Aryan flat. Danny turned up one day wearing blue dungarees and a workman's cap, with an empty wheelbarrow, which he had pushed through the streets of Prague. Whistling cheerfully and working at a leisured pace, he carried our most valued possessions in wooden boxes down the three flights of stairs, then pushed them in his wheelbarrow back to his own flat several miles away. Twice during the occupation Danny and his wife were forced by the Gestapo to move from their flat, and each time, at great danger to themselves, they took our belongings with them, to return them to me intact after the liberation.

Adolf had an even bigger problem: Pepička. After our deportation she continued to 'clean' for him, but each time she settled down for some hours of paid leisure, shamelessly making no attempt to work, only holding out her hand for the money. When Adolf drew her attention to the dust and the job she was supposed to do, she would sigh and glance around the room with a soulful look. 'So many things here to remind me of our dear departed Madame Hermannová,' she would say. 'How nice to know that you are looking after them up here.'

Adolf had no choice but to put up with this blackmail for three years. He finally threw her out on 5 May 1945, the day of the Prague uprising.

## 6

During the spring of 1942, the deportations continued at a regular pace, and still we knew virtually nothing of conditions in Terezín. What information we had came from the permitted thirty-word postcards, which we and others received from time to time, and from occasional fragments of news smuggled out of the ghetto, usually with the help of a friendly Czech gendarme.

The postcards were written in German and always began with the obligatory '*Ich bin gesund, es geht mir gut*' – I'm in good health, I'm fine – and then carried on with an urgent request for a food parcel. The ironic contradiction appeared to escape the German censors. More alarming was the fact that the cards sometimes contained veiled, often cryptic messages. Somebody had arrived at Terezín, but was not there any more. Had he died so soon? If not, where was he? If he had been sent on somewhere else *after* Terezín, did that mean that Terezín was not, after all, the final destination? That was a terrifying possibility. Terezín was surely a grim enough place, but it was in our country, within easy reach of Prague, surrounded by people who spoke our language and who knew, albeit from a distance, what was happening. If people were deported *from* Terezín, then in every sense it was into the unknown.

Around the same time we first heard of an obscure concentration camp, somewhere in Poland, which had acquired a sinister reputation for reasons which so far were not quite clear. Anything we heard about Auschwitz was based on hearsay and rumour, nobody had any direct news from there, nor did we know of anyone who had been there and come back. Why then did the very mention of the name evoke terror in people's hearts and minds?

Paul's parents were the first members of our family to receive the summons. They took it well, not succumbing to great panic. Paul wrote at once to Franta, who had been in the first pioneer transport and who now apparently held some accredited position in the ghetto. He asked him urgently to take care of his parents, if this was at all possible. After an anxious wait, we received his reply that they were well and settling down in Terezín.

Shortly afterwards, in early May, what I had most dreaded happened: my mother received her summons. Again Paul wrote to Franta. I went to the Central Jewish Office and told them my mother was an experienced nurse, and that if she could be employed in Terezín, her services would be very valuable. It was not true, but neither were the assurances we were given – that the Central Office would try to pass on the message. The remaining few days with her in Prague are a blank in my memory. I only know that nothing that followed was as painful as parting from her, letting her go, while I had to stay behind. On the day she and Aunt Ida left together I broke down in utter despair, for the first and for the last time. I could not even accompany her to the assembly point, and Paul went with her instead.

From then on I spent my time in a kind of limbo, waiting

only for the postman, but no news came until one day some-one pushed a letter under our door. It was a smuggled letter from Franta, which a Czech gendarme had delivered by hand. My mother's transport had been destined to travel on, presumably to the east, but during its short spell of quarantine in Terezín, he had managed to remove her name from the list. At the last moment the number of people in the transport had somehow not tallied, and she was included in it again. She had been brave and composed. There was nothing more he could have done, he was clearly distressed about it. The letter changed my attitude to everything: where before there had been a certain amount of defiant courage, passivity set in, resilience changed to apathy, hope to bitter resignation.

A few days later my cousin Martha was born. She and her non-Jewish mother, Cilly, were in hospital, where Uncle Hugo, the Jewish husband and father, was not allowed to visit. My mother had been devoted to her relatives and I felt that I should take her place. Without thinking of the dangers for all of us, I took off my star and made my way to the hospital. Mother and daughter were both well, and others in the neighbouring beds thought it strange that we cried so much. All of a sudden the ward sister appeared and announced the arrival of the official who would register the new births. A witness was needed. She thought it fortunate that a visitor – me – was at hand to fulfil this function. I would be called into the office in a few minutes, could I please have my identification papers ready. She bristled out, and I rushed into the safe anonymity of the streets.

In that same month the *Reichsprotektor*, Heydrich, was

assassinated. The news was received with stunned disbelief, hardly concealed satisfaction, and fear of the inevitable reprisals. We did not have to wait long. Heydrich alive had brought terror to the citizens of the Protectorate; Heydrich dead left behind a legacy of evil. The search for the assassins – Czechs who had parachuted in from England – brought with it untold hardships and countless brutalities inflicted at random on the helpless population. A sleepy unknown village was singled out for the most inhuman act of revenge. All the men of Lidice were shot and the women and children were sent to concentration camps; some children who passed the Aryan racial laws were sent to Germany for adoption. The village was then razed to the ground. Political prisoners in the Protectorate and in German prisons were executed in arbitrary reprisal, and it was no surprise that a special punitive transport of Jews was sent from Prague straight to the east, without pausing at Terezín on the way. The initial feeling of grim satisfaction at the execution of the executioner gave way to horror as long lists of victims were published every day. Our district was the focus of thorough house-to-house searches, because it was rumoured that the assassins had taken refuge in a nearby church.

It was at that time precisely that the lieutenant saw fit to display his peculiar brand of childish daring. He visited us one evening in full uniform. He wanted, he said, to discuss the latest events with friends. The Gestapo were searching in the nearby streets, but he put his loaded revolver on to our little coffee table and proclaimed, 'Now let them come.' It was a nightmare.

The Czech patriots were tracked down to the crypt of the

church. Betrayed and trapped, they took the only way out by committing suicide.

I went to the Central Jewish Office to ask whether anyone knew anything about the whereabouts of my mother's transport. To my surprise they gave me the address of their counterpart in Lublin, in Poland, and advised me to write there. They said I should supply my mother's personal details, and ask for permission to send her food parcels. For the first time since her departure I felt something like excitement and joy, and I spent hours composing a letter that would make the right impression on its recipient. I also enclosed a personal note for her.

The next weeks passed slowly, in a vacuum, with no content or purpose, merely waiting for the inevitable. When we received our summons at the beginning of August 1942, it was almost a relief, it galvanised our minds, and as we packed, dead emotions stirred again. I explained my worries about my mother to our old, trusted postman. I begged him to pass on any letters from Lublin to my Uncle Hugo, whose non-Jewish wife still afforded him some protection against deportation.

On our last evening at home our friends came, awkward and shy, bringing little gifts, not knowing what to say, but wanting us to understand that the forces that were shortly to separate us would not alter our friendship. The atmosphere was charged with emotion when very late the doorbell rang once more. The lieutenant and his wife had come to say goodbye. They too had brought presents, as well as a bottle of cognac with which to drink to our eternal friendship.

Somehow we manoeuvred them into the bathroom, out of sight of our other guests, and there we drank to each other out of tooth mugs, with the now familiar feelings of irritation mixed with gratitude and amusement.

Finally, after everyone had gone, there was one more painful farewell to be made: Adolf was waiting upstairs. One last time we sat together on the couch where we had spent so many hours listening to the forbidden news from England. We were spent and exhausted and found no more words to say. There was no need. Adolf wound up the record player: Dvořák's Cello Concerto spoke for us. We listened, we wept, we embraced and parted. We would never hear that music together again.

## 7

When we entered the big hall of the Trade Fair building on 5 August 1942, we paused for a moment to take in the scene before us. It reminded me of the Gustave Doré illustrations of the Old Testament, which I had gazed at in awe when I visited my grandparents as a child. This was a re-enactment of the Flood, the sea disappearing under the multitude of drowning bodies, except that here the human mass was floating on top of thousands of mattresses and suitcases. Our senses were overcome by the sight of so many bodies in perpetual motion, and by the eerie and yet all too human sounds that filled the air. But there was no time for reflection, we had to find a space for ourselves, impossible as that seemed to be. When we did find it, we disappeared into the anonymous mass that opened for a moment and then swallowed us up. It was then I first experienced the feeling of having lost my identity – my name, my past, myself. I was now BA677.

The noise around us was deafening but seemed to come from afar. The heat was unbearable, but inside we felt cold. Faces, some of them familiar, appeared and vanished again, and I began to feel dizzy and faint. It seemed impossible that we would survive the night in this inferno, but they kept us there for five days.

One morning we were marched out of the hall at gunpoint and lined up in the courtyard. After a long wait, when nobody knew what was going to happen, a small group of SS officers arrived and made a cursory inspection. Among them was an ordinary-looking man with an unmemorable face, whom the others seemed to treat with great respect. His name, the whisper went, was Eichmann.

After the long days in the hall, it was a relief when the time came to leave for the train. We were marched to the station at three in the morning, darkness hiding us from the sleepy suburbs. In our exhausted state we hardly noticed that we were boarding cattle trucks, and when the doors closed on us, we were only dimly aware of the finality of the moment. In a strange way our spirits began to lift, and a few even started to sing.

It was a journey of only about an hour and a half from Prague to Bohušovice, which was then the terminal for Terezín. Later, Terezín acquired its own railway station, so that trains could go straight from there to the east. From Bohušovice we had to walk for more than two hours, carrying our luggage in the scorching August sun. The horror of that march, under armed SS guard, was a fitting start to what was to come. Many collapsed and made their entry into the ghetto unconscious, on filthy stretchers.

When we finally arrived, half delirious from thirst and fatigue, we were herded into some obscure building, and left there for hours without food or water. We were in deep shock, barely conscious. When the doors suddenly opened, people arrived and we were expected to answer questions, identify our belongings, and take in a lot of information. Franta had seen our names in a list of new arrivals, and came to greet us and reassure us as best he could. A young uniformed nurse, who gave first aid, turned out to be my friend and fellow dance student, Hana. She promised to come and help me the next morning. As each of us was assigned to our living quarters, Paul and I were separated. He went to a men's barracks, and I dragged my case to the room in Q Street that was to be my new home.

There were about thirty of us in one room, lying on bare floorboards, an inch or two separating us. All we wanted was to sleep, but there was a poor mad woman among us, who crawled about on all fours all night, moaning and screaming and clawing at us with her fingers. I was terrified of her, and woke up with a jolt every time I felt her near me.

The next morning Hana called and took me to the washroom of the women's barracks known as 'Hamburg'. She stood guard while I washed properly for the first time since leaving home. This was forbidden, as I was not a resident of the barracks. I then followed her into the street, where she told me that she had a rare treat in store for me, a kind of 'celebration' of my arrival and our reunion. She took me to the ramparts, the fortress walls overlooking the ghetto which had been planted with grass and trees, and there, on the green slopes, I saw a group of young women dancing. I did not even try to understand, I just joined in. And so it was that I spent my first morning in Terezín dancing on the ramparts.

In the days that followed we new arrivals were given a great number of contradictory orders and had to perform a bewildering variety of tasks that seemed to have no other purpose than to break us in. One day, I had to sort out hundreds of empty suitcases, abandoned, stolen, or confiscated; the next I spent sweeping stairs and corridors. Then I had to take care of a group of old people, who, like the suitcases, had been stacked away in some attic and forgotten. There was very little I could do for them, just talk to them, pour them a drink of water, help them to the nearest disgusting latrine; after that, it was almost a relief to be back among the suitcases. And amid all this activity, we were registered, apparently as a new labour force. All our personal details – education, qualifications, experience – were taken down, and the farcical game of integrating us into the ghetto had been set in motion.

I still slept in the same overcrowded house, but the mad woman had gone, and Franta had put two nails into the wall above my sleeping place so that I could hang up some of my belongings – a few of the other inhabitants had looked on enviously. Paul lived in some terrible old barracks, and when we met in the evenings, we each tried very hard to present the other with a cheerful façade. He had one great comfort: his parents were still in Terezín, and in reasonable health and frame of mind. They bravely pretended to be pleased we were all reunited, but the reality was that they would have much preferred to know we still lived in the comfort of our old Prague home.

After a couple of weeks of this indeterminate existence, Paul was sent to join a squad of road workers, something which he found preferable to a spurious desk job. I was informed that in view of my background and qualifications I was considered suitable for work in a children's home. This had the immediate advantage of being moved into the Hamburg women's barracks, which was next to my place of work. I was delighted with my new accommodation, disregarding the fact that the room had no beds or bunks and was too small for the eight of us who had to share. We slept on suitcases, which was an improvement on the bare floorboards, and I liked my new roommates from the start.

The home for girls aged between four and eleven was run by two sisters, who were the superiors of all the helpers, myself included. If for a moment I had thought myself lucky to have landed a worthwhile job in a relatively civilised workplace, I was soon disillusioned. The sisters were not only inefficient, they were also insensitive to the needs of their young charges, who were consequently very difficult to work with. The children, quite a few of them orphans, were lonely, bewildered and often rebellious and hysterical. They were also permanently hungry.

In the first days after our arrival in Terezín, I had pronounced the food we had to collect from the ghetto kitchens to be so revolting it was almost inedible. By the time I started work in the children's home the quality of the food did not matter any longer, all I cared about was its availability. In short, I was hungry like everyone else.

Work in the home was physically demanding, as well as emotionally draining. We could never rest during the day. The hardest chore was to carry the barrels of hot soup, without spilling any of it, from the kitchen on the fourth floor down to ground level, where it was distributed. Every other week I was on seven days' night duty, which meant I had to sleep in the home and cope with the many emergencies, ranging from nightmares to bed-wetting, and from deliberate mischief to heartbreaking attacks of anxiety and despair.

42

The first task of the day was to search the little heads for lice, while taking care not to become infected ourselves. After that it was up to us to provide a programme of useful, stimulating and interesting activities, but proper teaching was strictly forbidden, on the principle that Jewish children were to be kept uneducated as a punishment for being Jewish. If the weather was good, I would take my charges up onto the ramparts, where we danced to the accompaniment of our own voices. All of us who lived and worked with the children deliberately and actively disobeyed the 'no schooling' orders, but we had to appoint lookouts to warn of any approaching danger. Even so, most teaching was done by word of mouth. It was too risky to entrust little hands with paper and pencil, except for drawing and painting.

It was impossible to restore to the children the feelings of security they had lost, and the one hour of each day they were allowed to spend with their parents only aggravated their sense of being abandoned for the rest of the time. We tried very hard to keep them mentally alert, to engage them in interesting, even amusing, physical activities, and to give them the rudiments of an education. But in spite of all our efforts, they knew very well that theirs was not the life of normal children.

Paul worked in the afternoons but was free in the early evening when I was frantically busy, bathing the children, putting them to bed, reading a bedtime story or singing a lullaby that might remind them of home. This caused us a serious problem. When at last I was able to get away, there was only a short time left we could spend together before the curfew. Paul now lived in a huge barracks which housed mostly young working men, and as soon as I had finished I would run as fast as I could to spend the precious time with him, sharing a bite to eat which one of us had saved, or enjoying a puff from a cigarette butt we had managed to 'organise'. He very rarely complained, and carried out his heavy outdoor work with a measure of pride I admired.

I found my work disheartening, in spite of the bond I had established with some of the children, and in spite of the friendships that had developed among the helpers. One day a new worker arrived at the home. She was slightly older than the rest of us, very intelligent and sophisticated. In other surroundings I would have called her glamorous. Her sense of humour taught us to laugh at some of the absurdities of ghetto life. She survived, and after the war became prominent in Czech public life.

An unexpected visitor called on me one day. Vlasta was a highly talented young actress who had already begun to make a name for herself. In Prague she had come to me for private tuition in movement. She was bubbling with excitement about a new theatrical project she hoped to share with me. Until then my only participation in the cultural life of Terezín had been as an occasional member of the audience at some concert or play. It had never occurred to me that I might take an active part in it. After all, I thought, who would be interested in an unknown dancer who worked all day and often at night and was permanently tired? In Terezín a rich and varied cultural life flourished in the face of starvation, disease and the constant threat of deportation to the east. The German authorities first forbade it, then tolerated it, and finally used it as propaganda to show off the 'model ghetto'.

A young playwright had written a new play in Terezín, called *The Big Shadow*, for an actress, a pianist and a dancer. Its unusual and controversial plot, reflecting Jewish attitudes to life and society in the past, and examining them, often critically, in the light of the present, suggested that assimilated Jews were guilty of both self-deception and betrayal. The central character in the play was The Woman, a part shared by the actress and the dancer. The music was both an accompaniment and a commentary on the action. Vlasta had been offered the part of The Woman, and remembering our past association, she had suggested me as the dancer. The composer, who was also to play the piano, was Gideon Klein, for whom a brilliant future had been predicted before the future had become unpredictable. If I accepted, Vlasta told me, I would be released from my everyday duties whenever I was needed for rehearsals.

From that moment my life was divided into two separate compartments: one in which I struggled on with the problems of my daily tasks; and another running parallel, where my mind and imagination tried to create shapes and forms, rhythms and images. Rehearsals were a challenge and a stimulus. The author himself directed the play, and I choreographed my part in collaboration with Gideon, for whom I felt a mixture of admiration and awe.

The play was a sensation and caused many passionate arguments for and against its controversial message. Some complained that the deeply pessimistic ending ignored religious Jews and Zionists, who still preserved their faith and hope, even in the autumn of 1942.

Throughout that time transports to the unknown east left Terezín almost every week. For most of us, the chance of being included was ever present. It was better not to think about it too much.

I was transferred to work in the boys' home on the third floor of the Hamburg barracks. The contrast with the girls' home could not have been greater. The supervisor was intelligent, wise and motherly and ran the home with dedication and fairness, as well as a lot of good humour. As a result, the atmosphere was friendly and relaxed and the boys were much easier to live and work with than the girls I had left behind. I often took them out to play on the ramparts. On these outings they walked through the streets in perfect formation, but once they were in the open they were transformed into natural, boisterous children. They shouted and sang and jumped, they rolled in the soft green grass and climbed the tall trees, they behaved as if there were no ghetto. It was difficult to calm them and line them up for the march home, and heartbreaking to see the sullen sadness return to their faces. Back on the streets of Terezín they remembered how hungry they were.

Between work with the children during the day and frequent performances in the evenings, I was expending a lot of energy, which I was unable to replace. It did not worry me, but Paul was getting anxious.

I was shovelling coal into buckets in the cellar one day when a voice behind me said, 'May I help you?' I turned and saw a short, stocky young man with a shy smile across an open face. 'My name is Raphael Schächter,' he said, 'and I have come to talk to you.'

I had heard of Raphael Schächter as a gifted and respected conductor. In the ghetto he had succeeded in gathering together a fine ensemble of singers and musicians, with whom he performed extracts from operas, or gave concerts. By any standards his work was of the highest quality.

He took the shovel from me and filling the buckets, he said, 'I saw you dance last night, and I knew that I had found the choreographer for my *Bartered Bride*. It will go on in the spring. Will you do it?'

I had to sit down. 'Yes,' I managed to whisper.

As he carried the buckets up the two flights of stairs he explained that he had obtained permission to mount a full production with orchestra, chorus and soloists. It was to be not only an artistic venture but also a patriotic gesture. *The Bartered Bride* was an opera with which Czechs identified passionately, but the Germans did not seem to know that. It was now November. Rehearsals were to start after Christmas.

# 8

Transport followed transport, both into and out of Terezín. New arrivals were greeted with that mixture of condescension and sympathy seasoned troops always extend to new recruits. The goodbyes from departing friends and relatives were quiet and subdued. What was there to say to people who were going on a journey, not knowing why, or even where to? The occasional performance of *The Big Shadow*, and the distant promise of *The Bartered Bride* held up my morale, and helped me live through each day as if there were a tomorrow.

A woman, newly arrived from Prague, brought a message from Uncle Hugo. It was a photograph of Paul and myself, holding the baby I had visited in hospital. On the back he had scribbled my mother's name, and the address, 'Luka Labour Camp, Sobibor, District of Lublin'. The good old postman in Prague must have remembered my request. Thanks to him I now had reason to believe that my mother was alive and working somewhere in Poland. Full of joy and gratitude, I obtained official permission to send a postcard, and after the *'Ich bin gesund, es geht mir gut '*, I poured out my heart to her, trying to fit all my love, anxiety and wild hopes into the thirty words that were allowed. I could not know the card would go no further than the wastepaper basket of some German censor, who knew that Sobibor was beyond any human reach.

It was winter now and very cold. People succumbed to minor illnesses, which in their weakened condition often developed into pneumonia and ended in death. Sometimes Paul and I received a food parcel, the half-kilo that was permitted. We opened them slowly and with great expectancy, divided the contents carefully to the last morsel, and then devoured every piece with a speed that made us feel ashamed.

There was a flu epidemic among the helpers and children in the girls' home where I had previously worked. I was ordered to leave my job in the boys' home and go back to help out. For the next two weeks I had to cope on my own, running the home and looking after the children, keeping some sort of order and pacifying the distraught parents. I spent my sleepless nights in the home and even had to forego my short hour with Paul.

After the first week I began to see as if through a thick fog and heard my own voice as if it were far distant. I no longer felt hunger pangs and my movements had become painful and mechanical. I knew that I could not go on much longer, and I became afraid. When some of the other helpers finally returned to work, I lay down on my suitcase bed and with infinite relief announced that now I myself was ill.

I thought I was just suffering from exhaustion, but persistent stomach pains and vomiting suggested otherwise. One of the two sisters from the home came to see me and pronounced that I was malingering. The following night an agonising sharp pain on the right side of my abdomen alarmed not only me but everyone else in the room. Next morning, a friend ran to tell Paul. He came at once with a doctor friend, who examined me quickly while somebody stood guard. His diagnosis was what everyone had suspected:

49

acute appendicitis. In normal surroundings immediate surgery would have been the answer, but this was Terezín, with its own peculiar type of bureaucracy – inmates could be examined and, if necessary, treated only by the medical officer attached to their barracks. As it happened, there was a lengthy inspection that day by SS officers, and every official or functionary had to be in attendance throughout that time.

By the end of the afternoon, when our barracks doctor eventually came to see me, I was half crazy with pain. He gave orders that I be transferred at once to the hospital for surgery that evening. When the stretcher-bearers arrived half an hour later, I was delirious but otherwise happy: the pain had gone. I felt a wonderful lightness as they carried me through the winter night. I could see the stars in the sky and talked to them, as well as to Paul, who walked beside me holding my hand. I felt that I was at peace and life was good once again.

I was brought to the women's ward of the Hohenelbe hospital. I was aware of white clad people surrounding me, and noticed with surprise the look of worry in their faces. They bent over me again and again, whispering to each other. I heard a voice say there was no time for the compulsory inspection for lice, and I felt a moment's worry. What if the children had infected me with nits, and now I was bringing them into the hospital?

I was on the operating table. An ether mask was being placed gently on my face. A faraway voice asked what work I had done at home, in that other life. I said faintly but with pride, 'I was a dancer.' The voice said softly, sadly, 'She will not dance again.'

It was Christmas 1942.

# 9

Consciousness returned slowly, and I became aware of a cold blue light and the blurred outlines of a human figure near me. I felt light-headed and sleepy, curious and apathetic, alone and protected, yet I did not know where I was. From under my heavy eyelids I contemplated the stranger, took notice of a white coat, and came to the conclusion that he must be a doctor and this dimly lit place a hospital ward at night. He had seen the flicker of consciousness in my face and felt for my hand. His gesture, both professional and gentle, helped to clear the clouds in my mind.

I looked at him more closely, and as I did so, memory began to stir and I said, 'You look like someone I once met in an office at the Jewish Council in Prague.'

'That was my brother,' he replied, and a link was established.

'Why are you here?' I asked.

'To be with you when you wake up,' he answered. 'Are you in any pain?'

My hands searched for the site of my former torments and found instead thick bandages all around my middle. There was no pain. Thankful, I fell asleep again.

I awoke into a new world of bright lights, soft voices, bustling people, and new pain. My bed was near the window and I could see the wintry sky and the bare branches of the trees in the hospital garden. Voices came closer and faces bent over me. Hands touched me, and the pain welled up into a crescendo that made me cry out aloud. Later I was told the chain of events that had brought me to this hospital bed, where I was to stay for many months.

The delay in the Hamburg barracks had caused my appendix to perforate. Peritonitis had set in and was now threatening my life. The operation had been a success, but its aftermath brought with it severe problems because of recurrent septic abscesses, which had had to be removed in further operations. There were no antibiotics, penicillin was not available, and morphia was in short supply. Instead, there was the unswerving, unsurpassed devotion of the doctors and the nursing staff, which was all the more remarkable because life was considered cheap in the ghetto. They all lived on the same semi-starvation rations as everyone else, in spite of long hours in the most responsible of jobs.

During the long, anguished weeks that followed, I came to know and love all those who supported me in my battle for life: Doctor Springer, the young, boyish, surgeon-in-chief who had carried out the operations and now regarded me proudly as his prize possession. He joked and teased, and never allowed me to see how deeply worried he really was. The even younger assistant surgeon, who came to sit with me on New Year's Eve when everyone else was trying to relax at some kind of celebration. The nurses who comforted me far beyond what duty demanded, and became friends and confidantes. And there was the mysterious doctor from another ward, who every day came for a few minutes and silently put a cool hand on my burning forehead. As soon as Doctor Knapp entered the room I sensed both his presence and a healing force which emanated from him. Later on, when I was a little stronger, he began to talk to me, and with infinite care and gentleness he introduced me to a world I had not known before: the teachings of Rudolf Steiner.

As a doctor, he knew how precarious my physical condition was; as a follower of Steiner's philosophy, he felt that he could help the healing process by talking to me about the spiritual life. After a while I began to look forward eagerly to his arrival at my bedside. No matter how naïve my questions, he always answered with tenderness and humour, and my slowly expanding consciousness helped bring me a much-needed peace of mind.

I thought a lot of my mother in those days, and of how she would have suffered to see me so ill and helpless. Perhaps it was better that she did not know, and yet I often felt her presence near me. I told my new friend about this, and he assured me that my mother was with me in some dimension of the spirit, no matter where she had gone.

In spite of so much medical skill and human effort, I made slow progress, and the danger of general septicaemia was ever present. My perceptions, however, became sharper than ever before. I noticed the fleeting look of worry on a face, and I heard the whisper which told the truth about my condition. I saw through the mask of Paul's cheerful smile, and I understood what my visitors said to each other when they thought I was asleep. One day, through half-closed eyes, I saw a man sitting at my bedside, weeping: it was Raphael Schächter. He had been told that the prognosis was poor.

I slowly made contact with some of my fellow patients, mostly those who were about my age and whose beds were near mine. Among them was Mitzi, who was recovering from an appendectomy. She and I were among the youngest patients, and so were naturally drawn to one another. I was still seriously ill when she was allowed to leave the hospital. I had liked her cheerful, calm, no-nonsense disposition, and felt that we might have become friends in time.

Meanwhile, a new wave of transports was sent to the east, but Paul and I were safe for the present: at that time the seriously ill were exempt from deportation. Sometimes news seeped into Terezín through the seal that cut us off from the outside world. Erica, in the next bed, received a card from a friend who had been sent from Prague straight to the dreaded Auschwitz for political offences. He seemed to have disappeared there a long time ago and had not been heard of since. Yet now there was a card from him, from a place called Birkenau, proof surely that it was possible for prisoners to survive Auschwitz and be sent on somewhere else.

It was spring. The tree outside my window flowered and I was still too weak even to sit up in bed. I could hardly eat, to the exasperation of the doctors and nurses. I concealed from them as best I could that I was keeping my daily hospital ration for Paul, who visited me every evening. It was sad to see that despite his terrible anxiety about my weakness, he could not help himself devouring the extra meal at great speed. Sometimes, to avoid his reproaches, I gave my ration to a hungry patient, only to feel guilty afterwards: I had deprived Paul of the food and had deceived him as well.

On a warm sunny day Doctor Springer decided that fresh air would do me good, and I was carried out into the garden on a stretcher and put under the tree. At first I was delighted to be out in the open and to feel the warm sun on my face, but I soon became afraid of being on my own, helpless and unable to move. I had learned from Doctor Knapp to seek the deeper causes of my feelings, and I now recognised that the hospital ward had become my true and only home, and that I had become estranged from the outside world.

The doctors decided to try a last, rarely used, measure – a blood transfusion. In Terezín it was an altruistic and noble act to give blood, and donors were naturally scarce. A theatre sister, whose blood group was the same as mine, bravely volunteered. She was beautiful, clever, and kind, and I had long admired her shyly from a distance. I was infinitely grateful to receive this precious gift from her.

The transfusion, made direct from arm to arm, worked, and soon afterwards it was time to make the first attempt to get out of bed. But when I tried to stand up, there was a new calamity which no one had anticipated. I had been lying on my back for months, with my right leg pulled up to ease the pain in my right side. Now, with two nurses lovingly supporting me in a vertical position, my leg simply refused to function. I could not straighten my knee or put my foot on the ground.

The profound, shocked silence in the ward was broken by Doctor Springer's cheerful voice, 'The muscles and tendons in your knee must have contracted. We shall have to operate.'

'Never,' was all I could whisper in reply.

Another doctor suggested alternative treatment, and was given two weeks to prove himself. For half an hour each day he came and massaged and stretched the knee. At the end of each session he just sat on it for a few minutes. The pain was excruciating, but so long as he was with me, I kept back my tears.

The treatment worked. A fortnight later, when I was again put into the standing position, my foot found the floor, and supported on both sides, I hobbled through the room for the first time in six months. Doctors, nurses and patients cheered and applauded. Some had tears in their eyes.

From then on I recovered well. I ate my ration of food and, as a result, was soon hungry again. I took an interest in my appearance and was thrilled to be allowed to put on my own clothes and visit patients in other wards. I learned to take the morning temperatures and measure pulse rates, and was pleased to be able to help the nurses in this small way. Finally there was a day when for the first time I was allowed to walk through the hospital gate on Paul's arm out into the 'freedom' of the streets of Terezín. It was July 1943.

# 10

After that first walk through the streets of Terezín, I found myself in the curious position of somebody who was living in a hospital bed while appearing to be fit and well. There was no question of my being discharged before my health had been completely restored, but I had become restless and I longed for something useful to do. Doctor Springer noticed my aimless wanderings through the hospital wards and decided that quite apart from actual physical care I needed to speed my recovery by doing something that would lift my morale. He therefore suggested that for a few hours each day I should help his much-overworked secretary in her office.

She was a strict taskmaster, but I was only too willing to learn. I studied the patients' registers and their medical history, I learned to fill in admission forms, discharge forms, and death certificates. I looked up the medical terms in the appropriate dictionaries and memorised them with care. I was introduced to the intricacies of doctors' and nurses' day and night duties, and I learned the tricky job of distributing extra bread rations to those who had worked overtime and not to those who pretended they had. After a day's work I would go back to my hospital bed and revert to being a patient.

And then it happened that one day the secretary herself was included in a transport to the east, and I was left alone in charge of the office, solely responsible for making sure it continued to run smoothly. I became a 'colleague' of the doctors and nurses, and came to know the real people beneath the professional veneer. I was happy to work with them and anxious to prove that there was a sound mind within my still very frail body.

My problem was that an abscess, which had been removed from my right side, had left behind a small wound that refused to close, and in spite of meticulous cleaning and bandaging, it remained obstinately open and suppurating. So long as it was treated every day it was not a source of any great danger to my general health, but it set up a psychological barrier in my mind. I imagined that it made me different from others whom I felt were 'whole'. At first I worried about it in silence, and then I began to ask endless questions. I was told it was a fistula, and it could be removed but only by major surgery, and no one would even consider that. Why not? I wanted to know. I pestered Doctor Springer almost daily until eventually he agreed to think the matter over. It was, he informed me after a time, a delicate and complicated operation, and one which he himself had never performed before. He would be willing to risk it, if he were quite sure that I wanted it. We finally agreed a day for the operation, fixed for about a month later. Until then I would continue as before, working by day and remaining in the hospital at night.

As the day of the operation approached, Paul and his parents, and many of our friends, became more and more anxious about the wisdom of my decision. I myself was weary, and unsure, but a strange mixture of stubbornness and superstition kept me from giving in to my doubts. On the afternoon before surgery – it was now December 1943 – I was working as usual in the office when Doctor Springer came in and told me cheerfully he would have to leave the hospital early that day because he wanted to go home and read up on the operation. He waved me goodbye. I spent a restless evening and a sleepless night: one by one, the other doctors came to see me, imploring me to call off this dangerous venture, telling me that it was irresponsible madness to go ahead with it. I listened to them all, thanked them for their concern, and asked the nurses to proceed with the preparations.

The operation went ahead and was a complete success in spite of all the gloomy predictions. I was on my feet within a week and suffered no after-effects. None of us was to know that if the operation had not been carried out, the open wound would have certainly turned septic within days of my arrival in Auschwitz six months later, with the inevitable outcome.

While I wrestled with my problems in the shelter of the hospital, the population of the ghetto had to cope with the cruel hardships of winter. Chronic undernourishment, poor hygiene and the harsh weather threatened the lives of everyone. An ordinary cold turned into pneumonia, a stomach upset into gastroenteritis; illnesses became epidemics, and an outbreak of typhoid fever in the children's home where I had worked caused many deaths, including that of one of my young superiors.

But people had also become tough and stoical, and encouraged by the news – some of it rumour – from the front, they were prepared to live on from day to day on hope alone, provided it was in Terezín. The real terror was the continuous transports to the east, where people seemed to disappear without trace. Uncle Erwin, my father's only brother, had gone with his wife in September. In December it was Paul's parents' turn. They left ten days after my operation and I was able to take a last walk with them through the hospital corridors. I remember that Paul's father, dignified to the end and keeping his emotions under control, placed his hands on our heads in a tender gesture of benediction and farewell. He died of pneumonia six weeks after arriving in Auschwitz.

Two weeks after Paul's parents left Terezín I was pronounced well and I handed in my own discharge papers to be signed by Doctor Springer. It was an emotional moment, which called for a small celebration, but my heart was heavy. I now had to give up the relative safety of my hospital bed and find somewhere to live, while still working in the hospital.

In the end I found a tiny annexe to a room in what had once been a family house, which now housed dozens of families. It contained a bunk bed, a chair and a shelf, but it was mine, and I savoured the long-forgotten luxury of being on my own. After months in the huge Hamburg barracks, alongside hundreds of others, I had appreciated the relative privacy of a hospital bed in a ward with only thirty other patients. And now I was suddenly alone and felt free. Free to look after myself and make my own everyday decisions, free to read as late into the night as I wished, even free to return home late, carrying papers that falsely stated I was a member of the hospital nursing staff.

In the caring, regulated routine of hospital life my world had encompassed a bed in a ward and a desk in an office. In my own tiny room I created an illusion of home. I decorated it with photographs, displayed my few books, and occasionally adorned it with flowers stolen from the hospital garden. When Paul came to visit, I played hostess to him, and we pretended to a civilised existence by eating our crumbs from a plate I had borrowed from the hospital kitchen.

It struck me from time to time that by being discharged from hospital I had lost my protection from deportation, but these reflections were fruitless and demoralising, and therefore to be avoided. It was spring again and even in Terezín the sky was blue and the trees bore fragrant blossoms. The war was not going well for Germany and people endlessly repeated to each other, 'It will be over soon.'

And then, in the middle of May, it happened: two big transports were called, and we were included. We reacted as most people did, first with disbelief and then with resignation. Doctor Springer and all the hospital staff were stunned: they had been so proud of my recovery and they had hoped I would be spared to the end. 'If only I hadn't operated on you so successfully,' he mused sadly. 'Even if you were only a little bit ill, I could keep you here.'

In fact, by the following autumn, even the most seriously ill were pushed into the trains on stretchers.

If we had ever thought that two years in Terezín had left us sufficiently tough to bear any hardship, the first few minutes on the train taught us otherwise. We travelled in conditions designed to inflict the greatest possible suffering. Old and young, invalids and babies were all crammed together so tightly it was impossible to move. There was no air, no light, no water, and one bucket. When the train moved out of Terezín station, many panicked, others wept, a few prayed, and most sank into silent despair. At night the train arrived in Prague and stopped there for a while, a long line of sealed cattle wagons, each with a tiny window behind a grille. There must have been people on the station platform, people who saw and heard. What did they think, what did they know, and how much did they care?

Another day and another night and there were few left in the wagons who were still in full possession of their physical and mental faculties. The dead were everywhere. Could one really pity them? I was almost paralysed with horror and had great difficulty breathing, but Paul remained steadfast and tried bravely and vainly to keep up our spirits.

At dawn the train stopped again. The doors were ripped open, and amid obscene yelling and cursing, some wild-looking creatures in striped prison clothes boarded the wagons and flung us and our bundles out onto the platform, where seemingly amused SS men with fierce dogs received us. A few minutes later we were divided into columns of men and women and marched towards the gates which proclaimed, ARBEIT MACHT FREI. And so we entered Labour Camp Birkenau – which was Auschwitz.

# 11

We arrived from Terezín on 20 May 1944. Until that day, we knew nothing of extermination camps or of gas chambers. We had been told that we were going to a labour camp. After the trauma of discovering the nature of the place, we came to realise that by some curious paradox it was not the living conditions that were the worst aspect of Birkenau, but that life itself was a nightmare.

In the shock of the first hour it was a relief to see a familiar face, to look into a pair of eyes that expressed the same stunned disbelief one felt oneself. Mitzi was a big strong girl with a practical streak and a sound mind, without a trace of hysteria. To see her in a state of profound shock was frightening, but also consoling. We had liked each other before, and we became friends in those first hours and days, when the reality of the place and our roles in it began to sink in.

One such occasion was when she and I stood together in line for the tattooing ceremony. Before Auschwitz, I had never seen anybody wearing a tattoo. I associated them in my mind with the heroic tales of the braves in *The Last of the Mohicans*. The actual tattooing was not painful, but there was a dreadful finality in the act. We also had to sign a curious document which stated that we were to be held in Birkenau for an undisclosed period of time, after which we were to undergo *Sonderbehandlung* – special treatment – by order of the *Reichsführer*.

Amid the soul-destroying restrictions and deprivations of daily life in Terezín, I had thought of home in Prague, even under German occupation, as a lost paradise. Now I found myself remembering the ghetto's ugliness with something like the same nostalgia. In Terezín, on the ramparts and in the hospital garden, there had been grass and even a few flowers. Trees bore leaves, or were bare, according to the seasons, and birds sang and called to each other. Here nature had died, alongside the people. The birds had flown from the all-pervading black smoke of the crematoria and their departure had left a silence that was like a scream. In Terezín people still had the recognisable features and characteristics of their former individual existence. Here, the inmates who had arrived the previous December had acquired a uniformity of thought and word, as if they had all been marked by the same inexplicable experience. They displayed a cruel, almost sadistic, urge to initiate us newcomers into the dark secrets of Birkenau, and to describe to us what lay ahead. The transformation that even the most gentle among them had undergone was frightening.

A short time after our arrival Paul and I were walking along the *Lagerstrasse* when we heard our names called out. It was our young friend Erwin. He looked dapper in an immaculately ironed prison uniform and wore his cap at a rakish angle. He greeted us with immense pleasure, as if we were meeting at a holiday resort. He asked if I had found work. I hadn't, but I already knew it was most important to find a relatively useful job before long.

The previous day my *Blockaelteste*, the woman in charge of my block, had offered me, out of the blue, a position of authority. I turned it down, pleading that I was not very good at pushing people around. She was furious and warned me that the day would soon come when I would regret my ingratitude. I thought of this when Erwin explained he was in charge of the laundry – he was in fact the *Kapo* – and that he could find me a job there if I wanted it. Of course I wanted it, it was an unusual bit of luck to be able to work under the benevolent eye of a boss like him. So I accepted gratefully and then asked timidly if I would be allowed to bring along my friend Mitzi as well. The request was granted and we parted as friends, or so I thought.

Work in the laundry was not too gruelling. We were to wash every item by hand, but they were all reasonably clean anyway, as they had been stolen out of the suitcases of new arrivals who had carefully packed them before departure. We then hung up the washed clothes to dry. Afterwards, they were collected and sent on for further use somewhere in the Reich.

Erwin was an amiable enough *Kapo*, but I soon discovered it would have been an error to assume we were the same people who had known each other in Prague. Our roles had changed in definite terms: the camp had given the insecure, drifting teenager a position of great authority, while the sympathetic hostess of long ago was now his humble employee, without any rights at all. My mistake was not to appreciate fully the seriousness of this role reversal until one particular day.

I was a few minutes late for work and Erwin caught me. He ordered me sharply to report to his office. There, to my amazement, he screamed at me furiously, then assumed a most threatening attitude. He was the boss, he said, he had the power to punish my slightest transgression; he was entitled to absolute obedience from me, I had no rights whatsoever. I listened and finally said, more exasperated than frightened: 'Erwin, for God's sake.' At that moment, at the mention of the name by which I had known him, he lost all self-control. He ordered me to kneel down in front of him, with my arms raised, and swore he would beat me to death if I didn't stay in this position as long as it pleased him.

It was an absurd situation and for a while I felt almost like laughing in spite of the humiliation. It was very painful to kneel on the concrete floor with my arms up in the air, but the sight of this crazed boy had a strange effect on me. I felt sorry for him. After a long silence I said softly: 'Erwin, you should be ashamed of yourself.' He glared at me as if he were going to kill me and then broke down. He lifted me up, crying uncontrollably and repeating over and over again, 'Forgive me.'

I tried to comfort him, stroking his hands, terribly afraid that somebody might come in and witness this grotesque scene.

He finally calmed down and started to talk like a distressed child – his parents had gone to the gas chambers on arrival, he was alone in the world, without a friend. He was afraid of life and most of all, of himself. We had been good to him in Prague and he had wanted to be good to me here in Auschwitz, but the evil of the camp had got to him, had taken possession of him, was working through him. He ended by saying he knew he would not survive, inside he was dead already. I said feebly, without conviction, that being young and healthy, he had time on his side, but he shook his head sadly. He did not survive, he never had a chance.

The September transport had survived until March, and then had been exterminated. The December arrivals expected the same fate at the end of their six months of reprieve. That would be in June, and our arrival in May confirmed their fears. We were to be their replacements. The September transport had had no warning, not even a premonition; the December transport had seen everything and knew everything. Quite a few had no intention of going to their deaths without a struggle; at roll calls and in the blocks Paul and I heard snatched words like 'arms', 'resistance', 'fighting'. We, the newcomers, were struggling with life, while they, the veterans of almost six months, prepared for death.

A devastating new rumour circulated in the camp. The fatal day was to be 18 June, and the victims would come from both the December and the May transports. Confusion and a deadly gloom descended on everyone. There was so little time left, and no hope. Yet, just at that moment, a light began to glimmer in the far distance: on 6 June the Allies had landed in Normandy. An SS man had let the news slip and the same evening everyone knew.

So far as we were concerned, the Germans reacted swiftly. The increased war effort needed more slave labour. Therefore only the sick and the weak, the very old and the very young, were to die. Everyone else was to work for the Reich. This decision, in turn, introduced a new word into the camp vocabulary, '*Selektion*' – selection. A selection successfully passed promised another stretch of concentration-camp life;

failure meant extinction in the gas chambers. Now a healthy and unblemished body became the only worthwhile possession.

My illness in Terezín and my many, many operations had left me weak and scarred in every sense. My abdomen was a mass of large, angry red scars, which used to draw astonished comments and questions in the shower.

At the first selection we joined the end of a long line of women. The line moved very slowly through a huge block to a point where the women had to take off their clothes and then proceed naked, carrying their clothes in a bundle, towards their 'judges'. Doctor Mengele and his SS staff asked each their name, age, former occupation and place of residence. In the time it took for the questions to be answered, Doctor Mengele looked over the prisoner's body. Anyone who displayed a blemish, varicose veins, swellings, discoloration, or recent scars was shown through a door behind the SS and never seen again. The others, the 'lucky selected ones', turned to another door, where they were allowed to dress before going back into the camp.

The selection went on for hours. We advanced very slowly. I knew I would not pass; for a moment I thought of Doctor Springer. Doctor Mengele and his helpers were becoming restless and impatient. It was all taking so long, and there were so many still to come. Their questions became shorter and sharper, the commands fast and furious. There were no more than ten or so in front of me when a voice shouted, 'Schneller, schneller, next batch will only take off their dresses and keep underwear on.' I was safe, for a time.

The next selection was just a few days later, to weed out

68

those who might have slipped through; for example, people of forty-five who had said thirty-five, fourteen-year-olds who had pretended to be seventeen. Another block, and this time we had to undress at the entrance. A line led to Mengele and those who had passed inspection were forming another line to collect their clothes. Those who didn't return had disappeared, naked as they were, through a door behind the doctor. Our numbers were much fewer than at the previous selection. SS men were everywhere, supervising the proceedings. I could not hope for another miracle. This time it was up to me. What did I have to lose?

Without looking at anybody, I took a giant step to the right that brought me into the line of those who had passed and were going back to their bundles of clothes. Nobody had noticed, nothing was said. I dressed quickly and hurried out to fall into the arms of Paul, who had passed his own selection and was standing there with many others, hoping and despairing men. He had not dared to hope too much.

A few days later he and I said goodbye. He was among a group of young men who were sent to work in Germany. Never before had a train with living people left Auschwitz, and as we talked for the last time, we spoke of home and a future.

Paul died in Schwarzheide Concentration Camp in April 1945.

The women who had passed the selections were marched out of the Birkenau Family Camp into the women's camp. The old, the sick, and the children, stayed behind. That same night the sky over the family camp lit up in a profusion of colours, from bright orange to deep red. We watched the flames that consumed the bodies of those who had been left behind. Paul's mother was among them.

Life in the women's camp was the ultimate in degradation and hardship. The sleeping quarters were cramped to bursting point. Soup was given out without spoons, so that there was the added humiliation of having to lap it from the bowl. Roll calls lasted up to five hours, and we were not allowed back into the blocks during the entire day. We did not work but had to remain standing at all times in our striped prison clothes, until we evolved a system of squatting down when and where we could, while some of us acted as lookouts. The camp inmates, mostly Polish women, treated us with hatred and contempt. They thought we had been pampered. How could we complain, they jeered, when we had just arrived? Didn't we realise that this had been their lives since 1939?

We were ordered one day to go to work. Work was carrying heavy rough bricks along a long stony path, depositing them at the end of the path, and then running back to the starting point. It was very hot and after a time the bricks became unbearably heavy. Our hands began to bleed. The guards watched, sometimes prodding us on, sometimes threatening to shoot those who faltered or stumbled. After some hours I broke down on top of the heap of bricks still to be carried. A young German *Kapo*, who was supervising us, saw me lying there. 'Get up and start stacking,' she shouted, first at me, then at others who had also collapsed. She showed us how to build a neat brick wall, 'slowly and methodically', then went over to the guards and told them some lie about what the wall was for. She kept this up for the rest of the day, and thus saved us from dying of exhaustion or being shot. Her name was Kate and she was a political prisoner. In helping us she deliberately took a great personal risk. Even many years in the camps had not extinguished her compassion and humanity.

By August many had deteriorated badly, both physically and mentally. We saw with horror and with pity how they let themselves go and neglected themselves physically, but we could only guess at their state of mind, because they had stopped communicating with others and were locked inside themselves: they had become the living dead of the camps.

A few transports had already left for labour camps elsewhere. There was to be another selection, for the rest of us, this time in the open air. We were to parade past the SS, naked, holding our clothes above our heads.

As I approached the SS officer, I saw that he was standing on my right, where he would have a full view of my scars. I forced myself to stare straight ahead, knowing that if he met my eyes, he would read there the fear of death. I walked slowly by, holding myself upright, then suddenly realised I had passed him. He had not stopped me. All went black and I fell to the ground. Someone helped me up and said, 'It's all over. That was the last selection.'

A few days later we left for Stutthof.

# 12

On the August day we left Auschwitz we marched to the station with heads high and a spring in our step. If we had been allowed, we would have broken into song. A *Kapo* stopped beside the line of marchers. It was Kate. 'How I wish I could go with you,' she said sadly, and waved us goodbye.

The train journey soon dampened our spirits. There was not enough space for everyone to sit, hardly anything to eat, and, worst of all, very little to drink. It grew very hot in the cattle trucks, and when at the end of a whole day of slow travel we arrived at Stutthof, we were again reduced to our former despairing selves.

At first sight, Stutthof looked to be an improvement on Auschwitz. The nearby Baltic Sea freshened the air, and lent a strange transparency that softened the outlines of the ugly buildings. We had enough room to stretch out at night, but there were no bunks and very few blankets. Accustomed as we were to SS guards everywhere, we were bewildered that they were only to be seen at roll calls. We were, in fact, left more or less to ourselves, with a minimum of food and water, appalling sanitation, and no idea of what was to happen to us. We sat and lay around all day, waiting, not knowing for what, becoming more and more depressed: we had survived Auschwitz, and now in this place we were doomed to die, lost and forgotten, of sheer neglect.

Mitzi became seriously ill with a painful throat infection. She had a high fever and was semi-delirious. A medical student said she suspected diphtheria, but here, as in Auschwitz, it was too dangerous to report sick – a doctor's surgery was often the anteroom to the gas chambers. Stutthof did not display its machinery of death as openly as Auschwitz, but it existed all the same and we knew it. At roll call we propped her up like a dummy, one of us supporting her in front, and one from behind, so that she would not collapse, and in between we nursed and comforted her as best we could. Without medicine, and without even a bed, she did eventually recover, nobody knew how.

In Birkenau, in the family camp, both Mitzi and I had worked in the laundry. We had stayed together during the terrible weeks in the women's camp and had arrived in Stutthof together. In those weeks we had become friends. Friendship in the camps meant sharing in every sense. The little bit of space, the little bit of food, the moments of acute danger and the occasional laughter. We gradually came to understand that this type of friendship was based on necessity first and on affection afterwards. To have a friend meant to have an extra pair of eyes to spot approaching danger, a voice to warn, and a pair of hands to support you when in need. When a true friendship developed out of this symbiotic relationship, then it became a precious tool in the fight against our desperate sense of aloneness and anonymity.

There was to be another selection, and again we stood in line. When they told us that they were only going to inspect our legs, I laughed aloud from sheer relief, and was rewarded with a mighty slap in the face from an SS woman.

73

Mirth among the prisoners was not appreciated. Those of us who got through were marched out, pushed on to a train and dispatched to what they called our place of work, Kochstädt, a satellite camp of Stutthof.

We arrived in the middle of a roll call and were immediately ordered to form ourselves into the usual rows of five. Suddenly there was a piercing noise, and the next moment the guards were chasing us into a nearby deep ditch. We stumbled and half fell, not understanding what was happening, but when the guards assembled round the edge of the ditch, pointing their guns at us, we thought the end had come. There was nowhere to hide. We stood crushed against each other. Panic set in. Many cried aloud, some began to pray. My mind went numb, accepted the inevitable. Instead of gunfire, there was that noise again and then the guards were screaming at us to get out of the ditch as fast as we could. They laughed when they saw our distress: it had been an air-raid practice.

On the next morning our new existence as part of the Kochstädt labour force began in earnest. At the first roll call the *Oberaufseherin*, the SS commandant, Emma, wanted us to know who we were dealing with. She told us that she personally had been instrumental in the extermination of the Jewish children from the Riga ghetto. The SS chief commandant was just the same, she promised, and we would get to know the others in time. On that same day our group also met with an unexpected problem: fierce antagonism from other prisoners.

There were three hundred of us newcomers who had previously been in Terezín and in the family camp at Birkenau. We came from Czechoslovakia, Germany and

Austria and we shared a fairly similar background and out-look. Most of the group were young married women like myself, although some were younger and some older. There were even some mothers and daughters among us. The five hundred prisoners who had arrived some weeks earlier came from Poland and the Baltic, as well as Hungary and Romania. Most of them had had a strict religious upbring-ing, which gave them a strong sense of identity, but sadly also manifested itself in their hostility towards us and their rejection of our group. They all could speak the languages of their home countries, but preferred to talk to each other in Yiddish, a language which I and the rest of my group didn't understand. They bitterly resented our lack of religious ar-dour; we thought them uneducated, uncivilised even.

There were, of course, exceptions on both sides, and we might in time have overcome these barriers had it not been for the one unbridgeable gulf created between us by Hair: we still had ours; they had none. Our long, dishevelled tresses brought their bald shaven skulls into cruel relief. No matter that our wild dirty hair, falling over emaciated faces, was no beauty and no adornment. They felt passionately that we had an unfair advantage and they hated us for it. They called us simply 'Hairies' – *die Haarigen* – and it was a long, long time before they would call us by our names.

When we were shown to our blocks, my friends and I found we had been allocated the uppermost bunk of a three-tier structure. This gave us a little more air, but, as we soon discovered, had severe disadvantages too. Our day began when a painfully shrill alarm woke us at five o'clock. This was followed by screams and abuse from the *Blockaelteste*.

Up, up, get ready, quick, quick, you have five minutes, you damned ... In that time in the dark we were supposed to find and put on our clogs and top clothes, straighten the blanket neatly over the straw mattress and visit the latrine, where there was space for thirty: we were eight hundred. Here was our pitfall: our shoes were on the floor along with everyone else's. As we scrambled down to get them, we bumped into the people in the second tier and bottom bunks, who were trying to find their things in the same desperate hurry as ourselves. Every morning this was a nerve-racking experience, especially if someone had moved your clogs and you couldn't find them.

Usually that left very little time for joining the chaotic queue for the latrine, and sometimes you gave up, hoping for an opportunity later on. By the time we were finally assembled for roll call, we felt like battle-fatigued soldiers, and, of course, it had taken us longer than five minutes to get there. To be caught late at roll call was an offence punishable by a ritual beating administered in the evening. Most mornings we were all a few seconds late, and as a rule a few would be singled out arbitrarily to be punished for the rest. Those unfortunates had all day to think of what was awaiting them. While we stood in the cold semi-darkness, guards inspected the blocks. Were they clean? Had the beds and blankets been tidied neatly? Were there 'treasures' hidden in the mattresses? Somehow they always managed to find some wrongdoer to be punished later with the others.

Sometimes roll call lasted fifteen minutes, sometimes an hour or more, and after it, at last, breakfast. Black hot water masqueraded as coffee, and with it, if we had any left, some bread from the previous evening. The problem was the same every day: was it wiser to eat your whole portion of bread in the evening when hunger was worst, or should you keep some for the next day, with the risk that it might be stolen during the night?

After breakfast, which only lasted a few minutes, we assembled again, this time in our *Kommandos*, work gangs. This was always a moment of great anxiety, because it was now that we learned which of the guards was to accompany us for the day. It had not taken us long to learn the difference between good days and bad, and those when our very survival was at stake.

On good days our guard would leave us more or less alone, so long as we carried out the day's basic assignment. We were allowed to talk, and sometimes could even stop and lean on our spades for a moment's rest. The guard himself might chat to the civilian foreman, smoke a cigarette or even glance at a newspaper, and pretend not to see if one of us dashed into the next field to grab a turnip.

Another guard might be a work fanatic. His ambition would be to get the best possible results from us and so he would not allow a moment's respite. At the end of these days, we returned to the camp, limping from exhaustion.

And then there were the committed sadists who had no interest in the work, and who cared only about the torments they could inflict on us. A favourite trick was to sneak up behind us and then take our numbers for an 'offence' they invented. Once a number was reported, you were marked down for a beating or for the return journey to Stutthof, where the gas chambers were waiting.

Our work was to level a hilly, sandy area, in preparation for a concrete mixer – The Machine – that was to spread concrete over it. The Machine assumed a sinister role in our lives. Sometimes we could see it in the distance, at other times it loomed large and menacingly close behind us, forcing us to work harder and faster in its shadow. If The Machine had to wait, the foreman and the guard became nervous, and that spelled danger.

After the morning shift we marched back to the camp for the midday meal. We were expected to sing as we marched, and we managed to learn a few tuneful and rousing Hungarian marching songs, even though they were in a language we did not understand. The meal was soup and your luck with it depended as much on the angle of the ladle in the barrel as on the goodwill of the kitchen workers. If the ladle was lying fairly flat on the surface you got a bowl of warm water with a faint aroma of what might have been. But if the ladle plunged vertically into the barrel, it came up with turnip, a bit of barley, perhaps even the odd potato. No matter what, we gulped it down and had scarcely swallowed our last mouthful before we were ordered out again.

Afternoons were hard to endure. After an hour or two our backs began to ache and our arms and legs grew heavy with fatigue. The autumn winds were sharper, and misty rain would drift in from the sea, hiding the pale sun. Soon it would be winter. Cold and worn out, we would be marched back to another roll call. The beatings took place afterwards, in front of the whole camp, and degraded those who had to watch as much as those who suffered them.

Anticipation of the evening meal was marred by worries about the size of the piece of bread we would receive. This piece of bread, with a dollop of margarine and a small spoonful of beetroot jam, was our only solid food. It was supremely important, and we thought about it for hours. It was not rare to find a woman shedding bitter tears because she had been given a smaller piece than her neighbour.

The hour between the evening meal and bedtime was spent in the washhouse, queuing, shivering, quarrelling, snatching the precious trickle of water from each other. And then bed at last, the shared blanket and a few whispered words with a friend. In the darkness, I heard hundreds of muted voices, some crying, some praying, some cursing; and yet, in the midst of them, I felt utterly alone.

Mitzi and I shared a blanket at night and every minute of our slave labour existence during the day. By that time we had become very close and a psychological dependence had grown between us that transcended mere comradeship in adversity.

There were at first five of us on the same bunk: Mitzi, Edith, Huschi, Annie and myself, but when the inmates were marched out of the gates of the camp in January 1945, only Mitzi and myself were still alive. After a brutal beating, received for wearing her stockings without permission, Edith had given up and volunteered for the lorry to Stutthof. In this way, she committed suicide. Huschi and Annie succumbed to exhaustion and weakness and made the same journey at other times. I met Edith's husband after the war. I did not have the courage to tell him the truth and said that she had been selected because of illness.

Sometimes the deadly monotony of our lives was broken by incidents which would, in their absurdity, have been in the nature of a joke, had they not always ended in terror and pain for somebody. How, for instance, were we to keep clean if the supply of soap and water was so totally inadequate? There were thirty taps and basins in the washhouse and the constant battles for them were inevitably lost by the weaker and more timid. So at cleanliness inspections they were punished for having dirty necks. It was a great risk to wash our scanty underwear, because we were not allowed to dry it anywhere and had to hide our wet rags under the mattress. Woe to those who were found out.

At the onset of cold weather we were issued with so-called warm clothes, made from some synthetic material. I had been lucky in snatching a relatively warm pullover with long sleeves. An older woman in the group cried bitterly because all she had been handed was a short-sleeved cotton jumper. With a reckless, generous gesture, I swapped my pullover for hers, forgetting for a moment that in this upside-down world an act of decency was punished, not rewarded, as I found out when the first frosts appeared.

We were each issued, too, with one pair of thick grey stockings. It did not take long before the first holes appeared in them. This was a serious punishable offence, so the stockings would have to be mended. But how? We were not allowed to own needles and thread. There were, however, a few secret needles in circulation which could be hired by the half-hour for a slice of bread. We pulled threads out of the blankets, which was a dangerous operation requiring skill and fortitude, because if you were caught, you were accused of having committed sabotage, a crime deserving the severest punishment.

It was at around that time I resolved to do anything in my power to be clean and I devised a method that was both difficult and strenuous. I waited until the last moments before bedtime, then snatched a basin with a little cold water and carried it quickly to the block. There I washed as best I could, ignoring the sneers of those who thought this behaviour eccentric, if not plain mad. Each evening I went through the ritual, hoping that this symbolic act would preserve a shred of human dignity.

One day, when Yom Kippur was approaching, word went round that to celebrate this holiest of days in the Jewish calendar the whole camp would stage a unique act of defiance: we would all fast for the prescribed twenty-four hours. Nobody knew where this idea had originated but astonishingly everybody, without exception, agreed and pledged their support. The *Oberaufseherin* was informed of our resolution and was naturally furious at such unheard of defiance. She responded with a counter-threat: if we fasted, not only would we work as normal but there would be no food at the end of the fast, so we would have nothing to eat or drink for thirty-six hours. The guards would be under strict orders to be especially vigilant for anyone who might slacken during that day's work.

We all ate the whole ration of bread on the evening before and ignored breakfast in the morning. The new, unexpected solidarity made us feel strong and light-hearted; we worked, and smiled when our eyes met. At lunch time the barrels of soup were waiting, and so was Emma, ready to sneer in case the sight of the soup should weaken our determination. We marched through the gate without so much as a glance towards the kitchen, and went to our bunks for a short rest. The afternoon was harder to live through, but though we grew weaker in body, we resolved to remain brave and steadfast in spirit. At evening roll call, something astonishing, incredible, happened: over the loudspeaker came an announcement: the *Oberaufseherin* had ordered that we should be given our evening ration of bread, as well as the soup we had refused at lunch time, and in addition – for the first and last time – a sweet pudding at the end of the meal.

We had won a battle of wills, but that was not the only cause for celebration that day. The barriers between us had broken down, and a bridge was built on the foundation of our solidarity. From that day on, hair did not matter any more.

As long as the pale autumn sun shone on us, we would somehow survive. This naïve belief, coupled with the overheard snatches of news from the front, helped us to keep body and spirit alive, in our race with time. But when the weather changed, with winds howling and rain turning into snow, our frozen and starving bodies silenced even the bravest spirits and clearest minds. We succumbed first to gloom, then to fear and finally we went numb. There were no reminiscences any more of the past, no more visions of the future, any future. All we could hope for was to live through another bitter day.

On one such day, a very young girl broke down suddenly and leaning on her spade, cried helplessly. A German army officer, who was just riding past on his bicycle, stopped and asked why she was crying so bitterly. She said something; he replied, and we noticed with surprise, from the corners of our eyes, that some kind of conversation was developing. Carefully we drew nearer, while our SS guard glared at the scene from a distance. We heard the girl telling the officer that she had lost all her family, that she was alone in the world and that she would soon die here, far away from her home, which was in Romania.

What he said next made us look at him in amazement. He spoke of the wheel of life that was forever moving; we, all of us, were part of it, moving with it so that those who were at the bottom could only move upwards, while those on high would by the same law go down and ever further down. If she understood that, she wouldn't despair, because clearly she would soon be on the way up.

It was miraculous that a German officer should talk to us in this way and it left a deep impression on us. The rest of that day was somehow easier to bear.

He turned up in other places, with other *Kommandos* from time to time, emerging suddenly on his bicycle, as if from nowhere. He always stopped, ignored the SS guard and spoke for a while to the prisoners in simple words that were meant to give them courage and raise their hopes. Then, with a friendly nod, he mounted his bike and disappeared again into the distance. In the evenings we talked of him, shaking our heads in wonder.

By the time our gang saw him again he had become a familiar figure, eagerly awaited by all. On that occasion a prisoner spoke of the immense distance that separated her – all of us – from our homes. He looked sad for a moment. He understood, he said, glancing at the flat landscape around us; he himself was longing for the blue mountains of his faraway home that he had left a long time ago. He believed that one day he would return and we must do the same; it was very important to believe.

A few days later, in the evening, a fellow prisoner, whose home town had been near mine, was looking for me in great excitement: she had had the courage to ask the officer where his home had been that he talked of so lovingly and with such longing.

'A little town in Bohemia, at the foot of the mountains,' he said. 'It is not well known, its name is Trautenau.'

She told him there was a prisoner in the camp who had once been at home there too.

'Please tell her to make herself known to me next time she sees me. I am very anxious to meet her,' he said with great urgency.

That was the last time anybody ever saw him. He disappeared as mysteriously as he had arrived, but I shall always remember the voice of humanity that reached out to us, from, of all places, Trautenau – Trutnov.

In late autumn 1944 two new SS women arrived in the camp. One was blond, pretty and ferocious. The other, Traute, was small, frail and dark, with an expression of sadness in her eyes that was not unlike ours. She was quiet and distant, and we soon recognised she represented no danger to us. Seeing her stand among us on guard duty, shivering and lonely, we wondered how and why this pathetic little creature had got herself into such an incongruous position.

One bitterly cold day I began to feel very ill and quite incapable of going on with my work. I must have collapsed in a faint for a moment, for when I opened my eyes, Traute was bending over me, looking distressed and asking what the matter was. I told her as best I could how I and many others were ill from overwork and from hunger and she nodded that she understood. She signalled to me to follow her into a nearby ditch and asked the girls to make up a little campfire to warm me. She and I squatted down side by side, looking at each other. It was a strange experience to be so near the enemy without feeling hatred, or fear or revulsion.

After a long silence, she shyly began to ask questions. What was my name and where did I come from? Where was my family? What work had I done at home and how had I become a prisoner in the camp? She listened first with interest, then as my tale proceeded, with mounting horror, and finally she broke down in tears.

The situation was absurd, bordering on the farcical, because I began to feel sorry for the distressed little SS girl. Mainly to stop her crying, I asked her carefully about herself. Her story poured out of her, revealing what I had suspected – she, too, was a victim.

Her home had been in Gdańsk, her fiancé was on the eastern front and she had not heard from him for a long time; they had loved each other very much and she had a baby by him who was now cared for by her mother. One day she had received an order to report for war work and had to say goodbye to her child. As a trained typist she had expected to get an office job. Instead she was taken to a training centre run by the SS, to prepare and indoctrinate her for her future duties as a concentration camp guard.

She was still trying to comprehend what was happening to her, when she was sent to our camp. From the beginning it must have been obvious to her and everybody else that she was totally unsuitable for the task and that made her position among her 'colleagues' precarious. She was desperately afraid of Emma, who terrified her, and of the men, who kept making rude passes at her, and threatening her when she did not respond. Our helplessness and their brutality towards us caused her great distress and she felt herself caught in an evil web that she did not want to be part of.

My stomach cramps returned and she became very worried when I told her that I thought I was ill with a form of dysentery. She advised me sensibly, if naïvely, to go and see the camp doctor at once. When I explained to her that it was more dangerous to see the doctor than to suffer from dysentery, she was at first incredulous and then horrified. I recognised that she still had not grasped all the realities that lay behind the façade of the camp's 'war effort', and I proceeded to enlighten her. She looked at me with such big, brown eyes that I felt I was being cruel.

The next evening we were woken up by the ominous 'Achtung!' from the Blockaelteste. We sat up in our bunks and I saw Traute at the entrance of the block. She spoke to the Blockaelteste and then walked towards me, gesturing to me that I should bend down to her. As I did so, she slipped a little bottle into my hand and whispered: 'This is against dysentery, I told the doctor I needed it for myself.' For a moment our eyes met and she smiled. Then she was gone.

The medicine helped me to recover, and thanks to Traute I was safe for a while.

Months later, after the evacuation of the camp, when we were on the forced march to nowhere, I caught a glimpse of her travelling in a horsedrawn cart with the other SS women. She recognised me, and we smiled sadly at each other. I don't know what happened to her afterwards, but I often thought of her, with the fervent wish that she had discarded her SS uniform before the Russians came.

One morning we found that a new SS guard had arrived during the night. We tried all the usual ways of assessing this new menace by looking as closely as possible at his appearance, the expression in his eyes, the way he walked, his voice. We learned nothing from our observations, except that he looked older than his colleagues and that his accent was pure German. That was better, we thought, than an Austrian or a Balt or a Ukrainian.

Shortly after, he took our *Kommando* out to work for the first time. We were always fearful and tense in the presence of a new guard and so I jumped with alarm, in the middle of the morning, when he suddenly pointed a finger at me and shouted: 'You there, watch out!'

Something came flying through the air and landed at my feet, followed by another sharp command: 'Pick it up!'

As I bent down, I felt very frightened. What cruel new trick was this? Why me? The thing I lifted was a small parcel.

'Open and eat it right away,' the voice ordered.

I obeyed and was staring at two well-filled, thick sand-wiches, something I had not seen in years.

'Right away,' the voice repeated and then he was gone, to reappear at some distance where he busied himself with lighting his pipe.

What was I to do? I hesitated only a moment and then devoured the sandwiches with equal haste and delight, aware of the surreptitious glances of the girls nearby. Nobody spoke because nobody understood what had happened and how it fitted into the scheme of things.

A short time later we all knew that something extraordinary and very rare was going on: every night this SS man kept part of his evening meal to give it next day to some starving prisoner. He always made sure it went to somebody different each day and always dispatched it through the air, as if to say, it is not from me, it is from up there. He did not like to be thanked, the gratitude in our eyes was enough.

As time went by and he felt reassured that his daily offerings remained a well-kept secret, he gradually dropped his impassive mask and engaged us in little chats – whenever it was safe. Those of us who knew German learned from him that he had been a teacher before the war, that his family was everything to him, that he was lonely and very unhappy doing what he had to do now. On one occasion he showed us a photograph of his daughter's wedding. It was not the bride's picture that fascinated us but her smiling father – in civilian clothes.

Naturally we hoped every morning that the Teacher would be our guard for the day, and not just because of the sandwiches.

# 13

It was one of the coldest days of the year. The November snow lay knee deep and a freezing wind blew unceasingly across the unprotected flat land. I was very low, frozen, starving, physically exhausted and on the verge of total hopelessness. The bits of clothing we had been given offered no protection against the harsh climate. The wooden clogs were always damp and didn't grip the icy surface of the ground. Slipping and falling could draw a guard's attention and had to be avoided at all cost. Being too weak to fulfil the required work-load meant a ride on the lorry to Stutthof, and the gas chambers. The lorry arrived empty on alternate Sunday mornings, and left two hours later with its load of 'passengers', returning in the evening with the same number of new prisoners so that the size of the workforce in the camp always remained unchanged.

The spade in my frozen hands was terribly heavy. I was well aware that I was only pretending to go through the motions of work so as to preserve my last bit of strength. Suddenly I heard a voice behind me. He had approached noiselessly through the heavy snow and must have watched my pathetic efforts with the spade for quite some time. The voice said in a quite matter-of-fact tone: '*Du bist auch schon reif für Stutthof* – You're another one who's ready for Stutthof – and then added: 'I have been watching you for some time.'

I wasn't surprised or even much shaken. I couldn't expect

to go on surviving when so many others had gone long before. Yet even that day came to an end and we stood numb and miserable at a roll call, which as usual went on for ever. A lively and friendly Hungarian girl stood beside me and softly cursed the interminable time we spent standing there, waiting to be counted. 'We shall have less time for rehearsal,' she murmured. That word, that once had been part of my daily vocabulary, startled me. I asked incredulously whether I had heard correctly, and she explained that by a quirky whim of the *Oberaufseherin* a Christmas programme was being rehearsed, with dramatic sketches, music, singing and dancing, to be performed for the whole camp.

I couldn't believe it: there I was, hardly able to stand upright, and they were rehearsing; I didn't know whether to laugh or to cry, but at that moment the SS man appeared and we were counted.

I survived the next day and the next, trying desperately to avoid the attention of the guard, but knowing it was futile. He had already taken the number stitched to my coat. It was only midweek now, three or four days' time, perhaps? The next evening we were ordered to dive under our bunks as protection from one of the rare air raids which took place somewhere nearby. By chance I found myself next to the Hungarian girl and again she complained about the interference with rehearsal time.

'How is it going?' I asked without real interest, only because she was so friendly.

'Very well,' she replied. 'Only the dance is giving us trouble, we can't manage the *valse*,' and she started humming it softly.

'*Coppélia*,' I said, nothing more.

'You know about *Coppélia*?' she asked with surprise. 'Then you know about dancing?'

'I did in another life,' I said, 'and I wish you luck.'

The all-clear sounded, she went to rehearsal and I crept under the single blanket with Mitzi.

Twenty-four hours later, and another day nearer to Sunday, we were woken in the late evening by the hated '*Achtung!*', the lights went on and the *Blockaelteste* stood at the entrance to our barracks. We sat up, 'at attention'. She looked at us, then walked straight towards me. 'Get up, get dressed and report for rehearsal in Block 2, within the next three minutes, this is an order,' she said and marched out. I moaned, got up, dressed and walked to the rehearsal block in great misery. To be deprived of even one hour of sleep was another step towards total exhaustion and collapse. The lorry was approaching.

Block 2 was well lit and pleasantly warm. In the huge room people were singing, acting, even laughing, and as I stood watching them I felt a sense of total disorientation and unreality. After a while I located a group of girls who seemed to be the dancers. I went over and sat down to watch. They ignored me and went on with their pathetic battle with the *valse*. A huge wave of bitterness and anger swept over me. They had deprived me of my only comfort, sleep, and now they didn't even notice me.

Exasperated, I jumped up and shouted at them: 'This is hopeless, you haven't got a clue how to dance.'

They turned on me angrily: 'If you know better, show us.'

And I did. They were first astonished, then became attentive and interested and eventually enthusiastic.

After half an hour the *valse* from *Coppélia* had assumed some form and shape. This in itself was remarkable in the circumstances, but what had taken place inside myself was miraculous. I had forgotten the time and the place and I had even forgotten myself. I hadn't noticed that it had become quiet in the hall, that the other rehearsals had stopped and that everyone was standing round watching. Finally, I felt satisfied: where there had been chaos, there was now a dance. The girls were delighted, there was a burst of applause and shouting; the shouting became a refrain: 'Dance for us, please dance for us.'

The trance held. I took off my wooden shoes, the excellent accordionist played a South American tango, and I danced. Where was the hunger, the fear, the exhaustion? How could I dance with my frostbitten feet? I didn't care or try to understand, I danced and that was enough. When I finished they hugged and kissed me, called me their 'star' and lifted me up on their shoulders. Some gave me bread and a bit of margarine and even jam. When I finally reached my bunk, I woke Mitzi and we shared the bread and then slept contentedly.

From then on I went to rehearsals almost every evening. The *valse* improved visibly, and I danced for the girls. They loved it and rewarded me with a slice of bread or a potato whenever they could. I hardly noticed that the lorry hadn't arrived that Sunday. I had another week.

After some more days of work in the snow, with rehearsals shortening my sleep at night, I began to feel very ill again.

I was dizzy from tiredness and my feet were swollen. At just that moment I was told that Emma herself would attend the evening rehearsal and that I would have to dance in front of her. Suddenly reality returned with a shock. To dance for my fellow prisoners and to lose myself for a while in this passing happiness was one thing. To dance in front of the SS woman was something quite different and it troubled my conscience. I tried to raise my problem with the other girls and was told that the *Oberaufseherin* already knew about 'the dancer'. It was unthinkable that I should refuse, and if I did, I would land us all in disaster.

I went to rehearsal that evening with feelings of dread and distaste. There she sat, an audience of one, seemingly interested in what she saw, applauding every number and apparently enjoying herself. They performed the whole programme for her, as far as it had been rehearsed, and kept my solo dance to the end. I danced the tango, avoiding looking at her. I couldn't have danced if our eyes had met. The dance ended. She didn't clap as she had before, but sat a long moment, then got up and walked out without a word. There was no cheering and no bread that night, and I went to sleep hungrier than ever. I didn't want to admit to myself that this episode might have some disastrous new result; it would be an ironic finale to my lifelong love for dance if it led to my ultimate destruction.

The next day was as unbearably cold as ever. We stood at the morning roll call, trying not to listen to the hateful voice that shouted commands at us through the loudspeaker. Then I was jolted from my frozen stupor. The voice had called my name, my name and not my number. It announced that the

*Oberaufseherin* had given orders that the dancer should from this day be excused from working outside with the *Kommando*. She should stay indoors, direct the rehearsals for the Christmas performance and receive an extra portion of soup every day.

The lorry receded.

## 14

The preparations and rehearsals for the *Oberaufseherin*'s Christmas show continued. She took a lively personal interest and allowed the whole cast and all the helpers to stay indoors for the last week before the performance on Christmas Eve. We wondered what kind of perversity motivated her. Was it some form of power game, or one-upmanship over her SS colleagues, or could it just be sheer boredom with her daily camp duties? We knew how very lucky we were to spend the days in a warm room, where we were able to rest between rehearsals. I was happy to have managed to find Mitzi a job on the team; she turned out to be a most efficient wardrobe mistress and seamstress.

SS guards from some neighbouring camps had been invited to attend the performance and to our immense relief all our fellow prisoners were allowed to come and watch as well. They even enjoyed themselves and at moments we almost had the sensation of playing to a real audience. We had to give another performance the next evening and afterwards we were rewarded with a surprise: goulash soup, with real meat in it. But the marvellous taste and smell were spoiled when I saw the hungry, begging eyes of the 'non-artists', who silently watched us eating. Even so, we were euphoric at that stage and became more so when we were ordered to prepare immediately a new programme for New Year's Eve. Something humorous was required.

We obliged. It is interesting that I cannot remember at all what I danced and choreographed on that second occasion, although I still have a clear recollection of the *valse* and my own tango, which had come to my rescue in that desperate emergency in November.

Eventually the 'good times' ended and I found myself outdoors in ice and snow again, doing battle with my shovel and spade. The difference was that I had had a fairly long rest and felt strong enough to face the hardships for another while. However, this time I was not put to the test. After about a week of outdoor work, we were confined to barracks, in the true sense of the expression. Some neighbouring camps had been evacuated and their inmates moved into our camp, which was now insufferably overcrowded. The new influx not only reduced our personal space to about a third of what little it had been before, but the poor, frightened women also brought their hunger and diseases with them. Our camp was ill-equipped to cope. Physical conditions were fast becoming intolerable, but this time we felt able to withstand them, at least in spirit, because we knew that the Red Army was now very close.

Two great questions remained. Would we be brave and strong enough to hold out until their arrival? And what would the Germans do to us in the short time they had left? We did not have long to wonder. On 27 January 1945 our camp was evacuated and we embarked on what we hopefully thought would be a long, long way home. The term 'death march' was coined much later, and with hindsight.

We were marched out of the camp in rows of five, leaving behind those who were not capable of walking. We knew from past experience what their fate would be and dared not talk, or even think, of them.

Some three months later, in Lauenburg hospital, I learned what had happened in the abandoned camp we had believed to be doomed. After our departure the sick and the dying were left in charge of a new commandant: the Teacher. He turned out to be an excellent organiser, as well as a caring human being, who put his ability and energy to work to save as many lives as possible. He succeeded in creating some order and bearable living conditions, where before there had been unspeakable squalor and chaos. He distributed the remaining food and medicines, tried to combat the worst infections, and most important of all, encouraged his charges to keep alive their spirits and their hope of delivery. This materialised within days in the shape of Soviet troops who arrived as liberators, as well as avengers. They were going to make short shrift of the SS man: but at that moment something happened that, in spite of its absurdity, was an act of justice. The sick women prisoners stood up for their SS man against their liberators, and persuaded them that they owed him their lives and were now responsible for his. They insisted they would not allow him to come to any harm and the Russians gave in and let him go, where to, nobody knows. I have often thought of him, hoping he made his way home to tell his tale and teach again.

On the march Mitzi and I stayed together and we were joined by two sisters, and by Vera, who had been alienated from her own group and was looking for friends. Vera was relatively strong, and her fierce determination to survive seemed an asset to our little group. That first day we marched still in fairly good spirits; we had each been given a whole loaf of bread and the mere sight of it filled us with delight and optimism. It was the last bread we were to see for many weeks to come.

We were escorted by the fiercest and most dreaded SS guards, who shouted their '*Schneller, schneller!*' as if they wanted to hear the sound of their own voices. The SS women and a few officers travelled ahead in a horse-drawn cart. At night we were herded into an abandoned church, where we slept on the stones. It was very cold and we were terribly tired, but we still had our bread.

After a few days of wandering on icy roads through hostile villages, we began to realise that we were, in fact, going nowhere; we just kept walking in ever-decreasing circles. If the guards had been rational human beings, they would have run away and saved themselves. But, instead, they stayed with us, faithfully obeying their orders to the last: to hate and torment us and in the end to kill us.

One night there was no empty church, no barn, no shelter anywhere, so we squatted or lay down on the road and fell asleep there, hoping that we would never have to get up again. I remembered stories I had been told as a child about people who lost their way in the mountains, and had lain down for a rest in the snow and fallen asleep for ever. No such luck for us – '*Auf, auf, weitermachen!*', no matter how very, very tired we were.

When the bread was finished, we had to rely on the goodwill of the villagers for a drop of soup or milk. Some gave, others didn't. With increasing exhaustion and hunger, we lost our grip on reality and our minds began to wander. Many of us had hallucinations, in which we saw mirages in the snowstorm. I saw a clean, warm bed near a window. Through the window I could see a flowering tree in a garden. There were flowers and books on one of my bedside tables and a tray with food on the other. I was clean and sweet-smelling, and my mind was at peace, because I was free from fear.

We were forced to march in these conditions for about two weeks. During that time we didn't change our clothes, and washed only our hands and faces in the snow by the wayside. Now we were past caring or hoping. In this state they pushed us into a deserted barn in the middle of nowhere. It was dark, but in the light of the open door we saw that the interior was made up of various levels covered by straw. This desolate place became our home for the next three weeks. The guards, except for those who were on duty, stayed in a nearby village. From there they brought every day a warm liquid that went under the name of soup. Nothing else. We were left there, to rot.

The liquid diet, combined with the grim, unhygienic living conditions, took its toll: the majority of us became very ill with a form of dysentery; another scourge which had beset us and now tormented us was lice. They were everywhere, in our clothes, in our hair, in socks and shoes, and no matter how hard we tried, we fought a losing battle against them. Once a day, when the cart arrived with the soup, we were allowed out, otherwise only when we had to relieve ourselves in the snow behind the barn. On these occasions, those who had wandered off in search of privacy were shot.

I myself saw the *Oberaufseherin* shoot a lonely little figure that had wobbled pitifully into the deep snow. She shot her in the back 'to prevent her from escaping'.

During that time I gradually lost the wish and then the power to communicate and share my thoughts with the others. In hopeless passivity I stopped talking, and withdrew into myself, and so isolated myself from everyone, even from Mitzi. The girls decided, and some declared openly, that poor Helly had lost her reason.

There was danger in this new development, because one of the unwritten laws of the camp was that survival was possible only as part of a group, never on your own. Recognising this instinctively, we all had formed ourselves into little units, where each member supported the others in all situations as best they could. To exclude yourself from your group was to enter the lonely path of the outsider, who could easily become a pariah, as I was to discover a short time later.

It was precisely at the moment when I had seemed to have reached the end of my road that Vera started to exercise an almost mesmeric influence on Mitzi. She clearly was convinced that in my state of physical and mental collapse I could not survive, and she managed to convey to Mitzi that any effort on her part to help me was useless and would bring about her own destruction. If, on the other hand, the two of them stayed together, supporting each other, they might both have a chance.

As time went by, many had become so ill and weak that they could no longer manage to climb down the levels of the barn to get to the door. They were lying in a long line near the entrance, their faces covered by their blankets. They were so very quiet it was hard to know whether any one of them was still alive. Many did die before long and were replaced by others whose time had come.

One morning I took my blanket and without a word went to lie down among the dying. I pulled the blanket over my face and gave up. A few of the girls who saw me lying there tried to talk to me, but when I did not react, they sighed, then shrugged, and finally stopped trying. Somehow I still got up to crawl behind the barn, but to queue for the soup was too much and I had to go without. From time to time I became aware of myself and my situation but more often I was lost in fantasies.

One evening, like a sleepwalker, I got up, took my blanket and climbed painfully back to my former place. I had had no blinding revelation, no inner voice had talked to me, no gentle hand had guided me, and yet I had got up and gone back among the living.

My former friends received me with indignation and scorn. They were afraid, probably rightly, that I would spread even more disease and infection and told me bluntly that I was not wanted among them. Mitzi was visibly uneasy and seemed to keep her distance from me. I wrapped myself into my blanket and went to sleep.

Suddenly, in the middle of the same night, the light was switched on and a hysterical voice screamed at us to get up, get dressed and line up outside the door, in no more than five minutes. 'We are moving on,' it added with an alarming touch of panic. In no time at all we had obeyed the order, were standing in our rows of five, were counted – even at that moment – and marched off. All except those who were lying at the entrance.

Much later, in hospital in Lauenburg, I learned about their fate. A few hours after our departure some girls, who were relatively strong, were promised a substantial amount of food from the SS if they did a certain job. They were bundled into a sleigh and driven back to the barn. There they found the whole row of women, murdered, bayonetted to death. Among them were a few who had been in reasonably good health but had refused to leave behind sisters, cousins, dearest friends. They had been allowed to share their fate. The job was to bury the bodies so that the Red Army would not find them. The barn was then burned down.

We walked, scrambled, stumbled, hobbled through the night until dawn, when we reached another village and another empty barn. I don't know how, but I arrived there alongside the others. Some hot liquid appeared and so did the *Oberaufseherin*, who walked among us, shaking her head and murmuring obscenities, which this time were not directed at us. The next day she picked out a few of us, myself – the dancer – among them, to ride on her cart towards our next destination, a half-destroyed house where we slept on the bare floor. By then everything resembled a surreal fantasy, with reason and logic lost. The guards wanted us out of the way, vanished, non-existent, but they would not leave us, and dragged us along to our and their own extinction. And we depended on them for the miserable single potato and the shelter at night, which only they could provide. We were bound to each other by hate, fear and degradation.

The next day was the same: *'Auf, auf, weitermachen!'* All day and into a night that was as bright as day, illuminated by artillery fire that seemed to come from a nearby field or forest. The battle was very close now and this knowledge filled us with desperate hope. The icy road was almost impassable. Coming towards us from the opposite direction was a long procession of fleeing German civilians, their cars loaded with people and stuffed with possessions.

In the confusion some of the women prisoners tried to break the ranks of five and escape into the fields. The guards fired but we could not see for certain whether they actually hit them or not. Exhausted as we were, many could not hold their balance on the ice any longer and fell. They were shot on the spot, in full view of all. At that moment my isolation from the group became a serious threat to me, because although I could not walk any longer on my own, they refused to support me. The two sisters understandably were mainly concerned with helping each other, and Mitzi was under the spell of Vera, who, as the strongest in every sense, had taken command of the group.

It was she who now declared that the group could no longer afford to help me along by linking arms with me, that at this hour each was on her own. In a sense she was right, not only was I of no use to the others, I was a burden to them, and as civilisation had abandoned us, we now abandoned civilisation and followed the law of the jungle, which says that the weak must perish. I can still hear her words, that night, on the final stretch of the icy road: 'She has had it, she is finished, if we allow her to hold on to us, she will drag us along with her, to her and our end.' And I can

103

still remember Mitzi's arm slipping from mine as she let go of me.

And so I found myself on the outer edge of our row, with no one on my left and no arm to hold on to on my right. Beneath me the worn wooden clogs slithered crazily on the ice. The road was congested and the column had to stop for a moment. On my left I saw a ditch, filled high with snow, and beyond it a house, a faint light shining through its blinds.

As once before, I knew I had only one choice; I took one leap towards the ditch and allowed myself to fall into the soft snow. As I lay there the door of the house opened. I heard voices, and the next moment our chief commandant came out, crossed the ditch within inches of where I lay, and joined the others on the road. '*Los, los!*' he shouted. They started to move and minutes later I was on my own for the first time in almost three years.

I got to my feet, tore the camp number off my coat and knocked at the door of the house. It was opened and I walked into a brightly lit, warm room where a group of German soldiers were having their supper. We stared at each other in amazement. I began to stammer in German that I was a German refugee and that I had temporarily lost my family. They laughed, and one of them said, 'We know exactly what sort of family you have lost, but stay here in the meantime and warm yourself.' He pointed to some straw in the corner and I sank down onto it, murmuring my thanks. They were chatting among themselves, paying no attention to me, but a young woman in uniform gave me some hot soup and bread.

Eventually the soldier who had spoken before turned to me and said that I could stay and sleep in my corner but that

I would have to leave early in the morning before their commanding officer arrived. If he came and found me, it would be a major calamity for all of us.

The soldiers slept soundly that night; I lay half awake, my head and heart full of conflicting thoughts and emotions. Several times I had to step over them to reach the door and some place in the open. Early on, as soon as they stirred, I got up to go, but they insisted on giving me some bread first. I thanked them, we wished each other good luck, and I was gone.

I struggled through the snow, keeping well off the road, and knocked finally on the door of a house. It was a spacious farmhouse, belonging to a Polish farmer and his family. They were friendly and welcoming and asked no questions. I spoke Czech, they spoke Polish, we understood each other perfectly, because we were all thinking the same thing: 'We are waiting for the liberators, soon they will be here.' I sat near a stove beside the old grandfather, and feeling safe for the first time, I took off my coat, displaying the striped prison clothes.

Without warning, the door swung open and there stood an SS officer. He brandished a revolver and screamed at me to get out immediately and join the columns of prisoners that were still moving endlessly along the road. 'I will watch you from the window' were his parting words. I was in the open in less than thirty seconds, and on my hands and knees I crawled through the deep snow in the opposite direction from the road. It was snowing heavily and I could hardly see, and when I finally struggled to my feet, I almost bumped into a small shed. I stepped inside cautiously and found myself in semi-darkness in the company of a friendly goat. I sat down beside it and stroked it gently. The feeling was extraordinarily pleasant. It occurred to me that the only animals I had seen in years were the SS's guard dogs.

I must have fallen asleep momentarily, for when I woke I looked into a pair of hard eyes and heard a rough voice speaking to me. The old woman said she had watched me crawling into her shed and that I should now follow her into the house. It was a cottage, where she lived with her son, Felix, who was slightly backward. She allowed me to sit next to the stove and offered me some food, but I was too ill to eat. She did not say much but kept her eyes on me. There was something about her that warned me not to trust her too much.

At night I lay on a hard, narrow bench beside the stove and listened to the gunfire close by. In the morning the battle for the village was raging furiously. Felix kept running in and out of the cottage, reporting in his childish way on its progress. 'The Russians are coming' – 'The Germans have chased them away.'

The woman spoke to me candidly for the first time: ' I will hand you over to the SS if the Germans stay here, but I'll keep you with me if the Russians take the village.' In each case she would do what was best for herself. After hours of fighting, it suddenly became very quiet. The battle was over but Felix hadn't come back to tell us the outcome. The old woman and I sat staring at each other in total silence. I was once again at a crossroads, but the choice of which way to go was no longer mine.

Then we heard the sound of heavy boots in the courtyard. The door opened and there stood a very young and very small Russian soldier who said simply, 'Germani kaput.' I flung myself at him and threw my arms around his neck. He looked bewildered and slightly embarrassed. Perhaps he did not understand that he was my liberator.

It was 11 March 1945.

## 15

The little Russian soldier left in a hurry and returned a short time later, accompanied by an officer. The officer inspected the cottage and told the old woman that the big room next to the kitchen had to be kept at the disposal of any Red Army personnel who might require it. She acknowledged that with a furious glance. He then turned his attention to me and asked in a rather formal but polite way my name, nationality and whereabouts during the last three years.

I told him what he wanted to know. He inspected my tattoo number and when he had finally satisfied himself that I wasn't a German spy, he asked me what he could do for me. 'Please may I have a cigarette,' I said foolishly and was offered a real Russian papirosa that turned out to be a punishment rather than a treat.

The next morning another officer arrived. One look at me was sufficient for him to identify one of my main problems. He sharply ordered the old woman to prepare a hot bath for me and to burn all my clothes. His men would provide new ones. These arrived promptly, clearly requisitioned from some house that had been abandoned by its German owners. The hot bath materialised in the form of an enormous barrel full of water and I undressed for the first time in many weeks. Until then I had always kept all my clothes and my shoes on – even at night – in case I would have to run for my life.

The sight of my poor, abused legs and feet filled me with

horror. Used from childhood to ski, to wander in the mountains, to swim, and trained as a dancer's most essential equipment, they had not let me down through the hardships of the last year – but they bore its marks. Blue, swollen and covered with sores from frostbite, they became very painful as I stepped into the hot water. I cried out, but the old woman ignored me, and taking her job very seriously, scrubbed me down with relish. She did, however, eye my discarded rags with interest and whispered that she would rather hide them than burn them. They might come in useful one day.

I was clean now and felt more human, but I was also very ill with fever. It was alarming, but I never feared that I might die of it. Dying was to do with gas chambers, shootings and beatings, the apparatus of the concentration camps. To be free was to be free from fear, even of death.

I spent most of the time sitting or lying on the bench, watching the comings and goings of the soldiers and trying to think in a coherent way about what had happened and what would happen next. In between, I fell asleep, and fighting off hideous nightmares, woke up with a feeling of immense relief, which not even the sight of my unwilling hostess could spoil for long.

A day or two later a very tall and dignified-looking officer walked in. He asked the usual questions and seemed satisfied with my replies: Helena – Prague – Czechoslovakia – Auschwitz – Stutthof.

In the late afternoon his batman appeared and asked me to follow him into the other room, the major wished to see me. I was surprised and slightly uneasy, not knowing what to expect. Nothing – nothing at all – could have prepared me for the experience of the next hour. On entering the room I saw a large table, covered with a clean white tablecloth, draped with the Soviet flag. The table was set for two, with cutlery, plates and glasses. The major stood there waiting, a gentleman who had invited a lady for dinner. 'I have asked you to share my meal,' he said. 'Thank you for accepting.' He called me Ljena. He gestured to a chair, and as I timidly approached he filled the glasses from a bottle. Then he said very solemnly, but with great simplicity: 'First let us drink a toast to the final victory of the glorious Red Army, to the liberation of your homeland and the safe return of your President Benes.' No dream could have been more unreal, no reality more dreamlike.

We drank the solemn toast and then sat down for the meal. I tried desperately to be polite and eat a few morsels of the strange spicy food on my plate. It was very difficult and after a while, I had to give up. He spoke Russian carefully and slowly in short sentences, so that I would understand him, and I replied in Czech. The dream persisted until he rose to take his leave – with a bow – explaining that he had to go on duty.

Back on my kitchen bench, I fell into a broken, feverish sleep, in which I saw strange images and heard voices calling me from a great distance. Two words – a name – were repeated over and over again – Donat Urban. It meant nothing to me.

Each time I awoke I was shaking so violently with fever that I had to hold on to the bench to prevent myself from falling off. In the middle of the night, the major returned, and seeing my pitiful state, sharply ordered the old woman to vacate her bed in the kitchen for me. He then lifted me gently onto it, and sat down beside me to keep his vigil. I was delirious and in terrible pain from stomach cramps, probably the result of the little bit of food I had eaten. Whenever I moaned too loudly he lifted me up and carried me out into the yard to push me carefully into the primitive toilet there. When I feebly knocked at the door he carried me back. This he did several times through the night. He didn't sleep, he just sat there, watching over me. Occasionally he laid a cool hand on my forehead and then shook his head. Towards morning the fever subsided and I felt slightly better and clearer in my head.

In this strange hour of dawn we talked. He told me his name was Kostja, he was an engineer from Irkutsk. That is all I remember, except a feeling of being safe and warm in his presence. In the first daylight he became restless and started walking up and down the room. He said that he and his regiment had to leave that morning. Their destination was Berlin. He was glad to be in at the final battle but very worried about leaving me when I was so very ill.

Then he seemed to be struck by an idea. He found a scrap of pink office paper in his pocket and scribbled a message on it. He handed it to me with the urgent request never to let it out of my sight or hand and to present it to any Russian I might meet: they would help me in his place, if they read the message. 'I want you to get well and to return safely to your country, Ljena, but I cannot stay with you any longer,' he said sadly. I watched him putting on his belt and cap and was surprised when he called Felix to my bedside. He made the boy promise on his honour to help me reach a place of safety whenever I was a little better. Then he kissed me on the forehead, saluted and was gone. When he closed the door, I felt utterly alone.

Kostja was the last Russian soldier to stay at the cottage. It became very quiet. Nobody came near it any longer. The old woman's hostility towards me became more pronounced as my dependence on her grew. She was not subtle in her assessment of my situation and she spelled it out with perfect honesty. She was not going to kill me or harm me physically. I would die sooner or later from my illness – as far as she was concerned, the sooner the better. By offering me the wrong food, refusing to let me wash or to support me on my frequent trips to the outside lavatory she could undermine my recovery. I began to feel hated again and a deep despondency set in that I instinctively felt could be dangerous at this stage – and yet, I made one more decision.

One day, when the sun was shining and the old woman was out, I called Felix and reminded him of his promise to Kostja. Could he take me somewhere in the village where I might find medical help? He readily agreed to take me to a place where there was some kind of military headquarters. It was a difficult journey through the snow and he bravely half-dragged, half-carried me until we came to a big farmhouse which seemed to be our destination. He opened the door, I stepped in and looked round with a sickening feeling of recognition: in the corridor, on the stairs – everywhere – there were former prisoners, most of them only half-conscious, lying on beds of straw. Russian doctors and nurses moved quietly among them.

As I stared at them a door opened. I saw a familiar face and in joyous disbelief realised it was the farmer from whose house the SS man had expelled me. Within minutes I was surrounded by his whole family, who greeted me warmly, asking questions, shaking hands, assuring me that this time I was safe. I was taken into their big kitchen, where a divan was cleared for me to lie on. I had found my way back to this haven. Kostja would have been pleased.

A Russian woman doctor was called. It was obvious she was desperately busy, so she just asked me what part of me was most in need of her attention. 'My legs and feet,' I said without hesitation. She examined both, dabbed them with a liquid and massaged them with some ointment and from that moment there was a steady improvement.

I stayed with these kind people for several days. They looked after me as best they could, worrying about my state of health and general lack of progress.

One day a Russian officer marched in. He was rather drunk and when he noticed me lying in the corner, he immediately showed signs of interest. I did not understand why the family seemed to be so nervous all of a sudden. There was surely nothing to fear? He spoke to me roughly, and not understanding a word, I just held out Kostja's message to him. It had an astonishing effect. Having read it carefully, he visibly sobered up, and in a much quieter voice told the farmer that he should try to get me to a hospital. Then he saluted and was gone.

The next morning was fine and sunny and so the farmer and I decided that I should try to hitch a lift to the nearest hospital. I said goodbye to my good friends, and we went out and stood at the roadside. He waved down a huge army supply lorry, loaded high with sacks of flour. The farmer spoke to the driver, who studied my pink paper, then lifted me unceremoniously on top of his load.

A quick thank you and goodbye and we were off on a hair-raising journey through a countryside that had been a battlefield not long before. I held on for dear life, in the truest sense, for I was in danger of being thrown off every time the lorry swayed or swerved.

Hours passed, and I was very tired and very cold when my driver stopped abruptly in a town. Across the road I saw some big houses with huge red crosses painted on the roofs. The driver lifted me off the lorry, pointed at the friendly signs and drove off. I entered a bare room where a number of people sat around, waiting. They all had the unmistakable look of former camp inmates and were clearly very ill. A white clad figure moved among them, a doctor at last. As he came closer I heard with a thrill that he was speaking Czech to the people. Finally he reached me and said with a smile: 'You must have just arrived. Welcome to the Lauenburg Lazarett. My name is Doctor Urban.'

## 16

Lauenburg Lazarett was a complex of large buildings, formerly villas. They had been converted into a hospital for the sick survivors of concentration camps who had gathered there after the liberation of the many camps in the vicinity. It was run as efficiently as humanly possible by the Russian medical staff, augmented by previously imprisoned doctors – like Doctor Urban – volunteers and conscripted German nurses. The chief medical officer was a Russian major, who was battling against his patients' deadly diseases and trying to cope with the shortages in almost everything needed for their treatment.

Doctor Urban was naturally anxious to help a fellow Czech as much as was in his power, which was not a great deal. He found me a bed that I had to share with a girl who had a suppurating ulcer on her leg. We were both very uncomfortable, but so relieved to be in a hospital at all that we didn't complain.

After a day or two I was transferred to a single bed in another ward and finally to a doctor who took a long time to examine me. He was an elderly, kind German who had volunteered to help in this emergency. He was glad to have found a patient he could talk to in his own language in this enforced Babel from all over Europe. From him I heard the word typhoid for the first time. It was a relief to know that the thing that tortured my insides did have a name and that everyone around me suffered from it as well.

They passed me on from one ward to another and I learned to gauge my own progress by the state of recovery of my fellow patients. The major insisted on medical protocol and he and his staff paid a visit to all the wards every morning. Among the immaculate, white-coated doctors was a good-looking young woman. One morning, after the doctor had gone, a young Polish girl burst into our room. She was upset and her voice shook when she asked whether any of us had seen the woman doctor before. Nobody had, but she had more luck in other wards.

Slowly the story was pieced together: the woman 'doctor' with the sympathetic smile had been an SS guard in one of the camps, and a very vicious and brutal one at that. She was posing as a doctor, perhaps in hope of escape, perhaps to disguise her past under the mask of the Good Samaritan. The girls reported their discovery to the major, who ordered a confrontation between the 'doctor' and the former prisoners. I heard that she was exposed and eventually confessed. Two hours later a notice went up in every room that justice had been done and the woman had been shot.

As my condition slowly improved I began to take more notice of my environment and the people I shared it with. Some were deeply – perhaps permanently – disturbed and depressed, others unnaturally lively, cheerful and talkative. Some complained all the time about everything, some were interested only in the food, a few were totally apathetic. They spoke Polish, Hungarian, Yiddish, Romanian, a few, German. Hardly anyone spoke Czech. Often they sang the songs of their countries and their youth and one haunting song they had learned from the Russian troops, who had made it their own. It was called 'Lili Marlene'.

I was already on my shaky feet and mentally much more alert when we were told to assemble in the hall for a special celebration – May Day. All the military personnel were present and quite a few patients and civilian staff came to listen to the speeches, watch the raising of the Soviet flag and join in the singing of the Russian national anthem. Then back to bed. A few days later, on 8 May, we were called together again to be told that the war was over and that all Europe was free. Czechoslovakia had been the last country to be liberated. There was singing and great rejoicing.

A strange thing happened to me in this hour: I cried. Big, unstoppable tears were running down my face. In the past year I had cried a few times, from fear or pain, or sheer exhaustion. This was different. These tears welled up from a depth of suppressed emotions and were cleansing and consoling, making me human again. I cried in sorrow for those who had died and from love and gratitude for those like Kostja who had given us our lives again. I allowed myself to cry in anguish about my mother and to think with hope of Paul. I began to feel my passivity slipping away and being replaced by a great longing for home. I wanted to get well and go home.

It was spring and each day I was allowed to spend some time in the garden. I sat under a tree, watching little birds hopping in the grass and listening to their excited song. I picked some flowers and held them in my hand and when I looked up I saw a blue sky without a trace of smoke. I felt these hours help the healing process just as much as the drugs and medicines the doctors gave me.

One day as I wandered through the house on my way to the garden I came upon a large mirror. I stopped and looked. The shock was like a sudden painful blow. The face that looked back at me was not just emaciated and white – I would have expected that – it was a stranger's face, dominated by unnaturally large eyes. I stared at myself in disbelief. I was liberated, safe, hopeful of a new life, yet that face was marked with an expression of such intense suffering and anguish that I recoiled from it, wanting to disown it. I stood for a long time staring, trying to find a trace of my former self in this mask, until I had to admit that I had been used to seeing these sad faces all around, but naïvely or arrogantly I had assumed that mine would be different. Would time give me back my face, or would it bear the mark of the camps for life, like the tattoo on my left forearm?

After that, my daily bath became an obsessive ritual. I spent hours soaking in the water, washing and scrubbing myself, as if by doing so I could wash away the past and give myself a new face. Eventually the nurses warned me that too much hot water for too long a time was dangerous to my precarious state of health.

Some days I felt strong enough to plan a future, only to be reminded at other times of my frailty. There was the incident with the cocoa. It arrived in our room unannounced, in a big steaming jug, and its smell filled us with happy anticipation. My bed was near the door and when the jug had made its round, there was none left for me. I cried bitterly, like a baby, and couldn't stop in spite of feeling thoroughly ashamed of myself.

I rediscovered the delight of books. There was not much

choice, but I renewed my love for Theodor Storm by reading *Der Schimmelreiter* again and I devoured a wonderful biography of Michelangelo, I think by Heinrich Mann. They were my first intellectual nourishment in a long time.

The day came when Doctor Urban came to say goodbye, he was going home to Prague. I never saw him again.

Towards the end of May alarming rumours disturbed the peace of our convalescence: the Soviet Union planned to annex permanently the north-eastern part of Poland, including Pomerania, and we might then encounter great difficulties in getting home. Quite a few people panicked, I among them. I had previously met a Czech woman, Annie, who was ready to leave and suggested we should travel together if I could procure my medical discharge. This was not as easy as I had imagined. The woman doctor in charge warned me of the dangers of such a long journey in my fragile state of health. I insisted and in the end she agreed to sign my release papers on condition that I signed a document declaring I had left the hospital of my own free will and against the advice of the medical officer.

And so we left. After a few hours' train journey we arrived at Bydgoszcz, where we had to report to the local repatriation office. We were given some provisions, money and a few pieces of well-meant but useless advice on how to travel in a country where hardly any transport was left intact.

The next train took us a stage further until it just stopped. We got out and waited for hours at the railway station for another. This happened several times. There were no timetables, no tickets, no railway personnel. We had to find out whether a train was travelling west and if so, get on it. This involved an enormous effort: pushing through the often hysterical crowds, climbing the steps on to the trains and finding some place to stand, sit or squat, and all without losing each other. I remembered the Lauenburg doctor's warning.

In one of the dilapidated railway stations we shared a bench with a Pole, who, like us, bore the marks of the camps. He was eager to talk and to ask and answer questions. I forced myself to ask him: 'What do you know of Sobibor?' He buried his head in his hands and I saw that he was shaking. 'Don't ask about Sobibor,' he said. 'Don't even speak its name.' I knew then.

At each stage of our journey home we were guided by signs displaying the names of big stations we recognised: Poznań, Częstochowa, Katowice. At least we knew where we were on the map.

An exciting encounter in Poznań cheered me up tremendously. In an enormous railway hall teeming with ill-tempered and lost refugees, I ran into the Hungarian girl who in Kochstädt had hummed *Coppélia* to me. There was time only for a short embrace, a few questions and answers and some heartfelt wishes for the future. But it was so good to know that she, too, was alive and on her way home.

At last we arrived in Katowice. We walked through the half-destroyed town to the repatriation office. This time we were issued with three hundred crowns and a travel document with our personal details.

Towards the evening of the fifth day we finally reached the Czechoslovakian border, only to be told that the train wasn't going any further. We spent that night in exhausted sleep in an abandoned railway carriage, in the no-man's-land between the two countries. A Yugoslav family, who were also trying to find their way home, told us the next day that there had been drunken Russian soldiers roaming the vicinity, looking for women. They had managed to divert their attention from our carriage.

Suddenly, out of the blue, a single locomotive appeared, like a ghost out of the mist. The driver allowed us to join him in his cab and from this elevated position we got our first glimpse of Moravská Ostrava. Walking through the streets, we saw posters everywhere, telling in triumphant tones the story of the destruction of Dresden four months previously, which, of course, was news to us. We managed to catch a train to Prostějov, where again we had to wait endless hours. Finally, with feelings that cannot be described, we boarded a coach with Praha – Prague – painted on it.

It was an ordinary, crowded passenger train, with ordinary passengers, who at first looked at us out of the corner of their eyes. The more sensitive looked away when they realised who their strange-looking fellow passengers were, others stared with naked curiosity, others pretended not to see. Few spoke.

I sat beside a man who was reading a newspaper. Peeping over his shoulder, I found that the name Truman appeared several times prominently on the front page. Summoning up my courage, I asked who that was. He gave me a long look, shook his head disapprovingly and informed me loudly that Truman was the president of the United States, as everyone knew or ought to know. I was surprised. What had happened to Roosevelt? But I did not like to ask.

At midnight we arrived in Prague, at Wilson Station. We almost fell out of the train and with our last strength made our way to the Red Cross Centre in the station. The night nurse was just about to pack up. We begged her for a cup of tea, but she said there was none at that hour. We told her where we had come from.

'How long were you in the concentration camp?' she asked.

'Three years.'

'Well if you stuck it out there for three years, you'll survive one night without tea,' she said and closed up.

Outside, the city was under curfew, so we bedded down on the stone floor of the station and there spent our first night at home.

It was 4 June 1945.

## 17

The next morning, after a shower in the grimy underground washroom in the station, we felt able to face the streets of Prague. My first impression was of shock and disorientation. Everything was as I remembered it – busy streets, lots of people, traffic, noise. But how did I fit into it? Was there a place for me in this continuing, unchanging world? Annie and I said goodbye, but I hesitated for a long time before boarding a tram, where I discovered that 'homecomers' like myself did not have to pay the fare.

The house where Uncle Hugo and Aunt Cilly lived was intact, and his nameplate was still there at the entrance, among all the others. I found the courage to press the bell, but when he answered, I could only whisper my name. The automatic door opened, I went in and collapsed in a faint outside the lift. Aunt Cilly, who had been out shopping, found me there a few moments later. She did not recognise me till I opened my eyes and spoke her name.

Cilly and Hugo were naturally delighted that I was alive and had returned, but they could not hide their dismay at my appearance. Two and a half months after my liberation my weight was still only thirty kilos, and I was in rags. They said they wanted me to stay with them, although their flat, which to me seemed of luxurious proportions, was in fact far too small for a family of four and myself. Never mind, a mattress in a corner was all I needed and wanted.

Finally the dreaded moment came, when I could no longer delay asking, 'Where is . . . ?' 'Any news of . . . ?' 'Any hope for . . . ?' The answers were simple: those of the family who had lived in so-called mixed marriages had survived, the others had not. My Aunt Tilly and Uncle Alfi, from my father's side of the family, belonged to the first category and had returned from their respective imprisonments to their home in Mladá Boleslav.

Hugo asked carefully about my mother. I told them what I knew about Sobibor, the place from where nobody had ever returned. We sat in silence until Cilly fetched a postcard, and gave it to me with a smile: it was from Paul, written in Schwarzheide on 15 March 1945. It said that he was well and would be grateful for a food parcel. He did not know the whereabouts of his wife and mother. The handwriting was firm and clear, and looking again at the date, I felt a strong hope that he was alive and perhaps on his way home.

It was not easy for Hugo and Cilly to adjust to my presence, nor for me to fit in to their family life. None of us quite understood that I was still far from well, and that physically and psychologically I was in need of treatment and help. The proper place for me would have been a convalescent home, but I had an almost pathological fear of any kind of institution where I might be detained and deprived of my freedom of movement. It was all-important to me to be able to come and go at will, to meet whomever I wanted to see, and to answer for my actions to no one but myself. When I went to see my friends, I was touched by the love and kindness with which they welcomed me back and by their willingness to help me.

Someone told me about the repatriation office in the Old Town, where information could be obtained about former prisoners who had been located since the end of the war. I made my way there every day, in the hope of news of Paul. It was a long journey across town by tram and on foot. No news. One day, as I stood tired and dejected at the tram stop, I heard a cheerful voice call my name. It was a young man whom we had known in Terezín, and who was delighted to see me alive.

We chatted for a moment, and then he said, 'You know, I was with Paul to the last moment.'

'What last moment?' I asked.

He shook his head. 'He seemed to be all right in the evening, but in the morning he was gone.'

'Gone where?' I asked.

'He was dead,' he said.

I stared at him, and he realised that I had not known of Paul's death, and panicked. 'Excuse me, here is my tram,' he exclaimed, and left me standing there.

I desperately needed a quiet corner to myself, where I could sit and contemplate whether and how to go on with my life. A kind friend offered me a room in her spacious flat. I was grateful for the privacy and to be allowed to give in to the sadness that enveloped me.

One morning about a week later the doorbell rang, and there stood Tilly and Alfi. 'Get dressed and pack your things, we are going home to Mladá Boleslav,' they said firmly.

Tilly had spent the last six months of the war in Terezín, while Alfi had been in a camp for Aryan husbands whose crime it was not to have forsaken their Jewish wives. After their return and happy reunion, they faced a new problem: Alfi was German and spoke Czech with a heavy accent. He was safe in Mladá Boleslav, where everyone knew about his exemplary behaviour, but elsewhere he was at risk. In those days of fierce anti-German feelings a train journey could be hazardous for him. I had written to them of Paul's death, and they had waved their fears aside and come to my help.

On the train my pathetic appearance served as a protective shield for Alfi. In Mladá Boleslav, I had space, quiet, loving care and understanding company, when I wanted it, everything, in fact, except my health and strength. In their anxiety to help, Tilly and Alfi took me to Doctor Springer, who was in Terezín to wind up the health department. He hugged and kissed me like a child who had found a precious toy that had been feared lost. He examined me, then happily declared that Tilly and Alfi should not worry too much, he was sure I would survive this crisis like all the others before.

We also went to Trutnov. There in the streets I met the strange and ironic spectacle of people with red or white armbands. The white ones were former Nazis who were later to be expelled, the few red ones, Nazi opponents who were allowed to stay. I went to see Gusti, and in her arms found peace of mind for a while. She told me that she had always known I would return one day, she had never doubted it; as proof she produced some home-made raspberry juice which she had made specially for me because I had loved it so much as a child.

The juice was as good as ever, but it made me violently sick. That was the problem. I could not retain the food that

Tilly unfailingly prepared for me, vitamins had no effect, and the local doctor became concerned about my lack of progress. When I developed some painful abscesses, I had no choice but to agree to go into hospital as an in-patient. The doctors and nursing staff were kind and efficient, but I was aloof, despondent, and uncooperative. The surgeon had an idea: he brought in a doctor who had himself been in the camps, and now specialised in the treatment of former in-mates. He examined me, and we had a long talk; he recommended that my bed should be screened off for a time, and prescribed special baths and a new diet. The new regime worked, and I slowly began to get better. I started to eat the hospital meals as well as Tilly's lovingly prepared home cooking, and as I gained physical strength, I gradually emerged from my depression and apathy. I read books again, and wrote to friends and relatives in Prague. They, in turn, wrote me letters of encouragement and hope that I would return to them soon.

One of these letters from my friend Hana brought back the pain of the past with some astonishing news about Mitzi. I had heard in Prague that the other four of our group had survived the death march and made their way home, but in my state of despondency I did not care. I thought of Mitzi only with a vague sadness and without any wish ever to see her again. Hana wrote that she and Mitzi had met by chance. When my name came up in conversation, Mitzi had become very agitated. She showed Hana a scar on her forearm and told her with tears in her eyes that she had been shot at by an SS man while she held me dying in her arms. This scar would forever remind her of my last moments. Hana was

127

incredulous. She had had my letter from Mladá Boleslav only a few days before. In it I had said that I was slowly recovering.

I was badly shaken by that story, and in the darker corners of my mind lurked a vague idea of revenge and retribution. I began to think of it seriously, when later, after my return to Prague in the spring of 1946, I realised on several occasions that Mitzi's sob story of friendship unto death had made the rounds. Once I had to support a lady who was about to faint when she thought she had seen my ghost hanging on to a strap in a tram.

The inevitable happened – Mitzi and I found ourselves face to face, in the anteroom of some government office. I had imagined that meeting so often that when it happened it was an anticlimax. I had played with the thought of it with a certain amount of righteous *Schadenfreude*; to her, the same thought must have been a cruel nightmare. In the event there was no great drama. We went for coffee and talked for a long time: she, about her dreadful feelings of guilt; I, about my equally painful feelings of abandonment. What she told me was the epilogue to her story and mine.

When she and the others on the march realised I had disappeared, they did naturally assume that I had fallen and been shot. The following morning they were liberated by the Red Army. Most of them were seriously ill, suffering from dysentery and typhoid. In her feverish hallucinations Mitzi imagined what she later related as fact. A painful wound on her arm became connected with my sudden disappearance and helped her to overcome her feelings of guilt for the part she had played in my presumed death. What she imagined in her feverish dreams became a reality in which she fervently wanted to believe. It had never entered her mind that I might actually have survived.

In the end we understood each other, but when she pleaded that we should meet again, I had to say no. Shortly afterwards she emigrated to Australia.

The day came when I was finally declared well enough to be discharged from hospital. Tilly came to fetch me and I noticed a happy twinkle in her eye. 'I have a surprise for you,' she said. It was a letter from Harry, from that faraway city in foreign lands, Belfast.

It was October 1945.

Helen Lewis's journey home to Prague
after her liberation in 1945

Harry and I were married in the beautiful Old Town Hall in Prague in June 1947. Before that I had been working part time in Prague as a foreign language secretary. I had had to admit to myself that I was still not strong enough to hope for a career in dance again and I considered, with sadness, that chapter in my life closed.

I arrived in Belfast at the end of October and spent the first two years learning to understand that strange place, its language, customs and people. Harry guided me along with tact, patience and good humour. Yet in spite of being safe and feeling secure, I was tormented by a recurring nightmare, from which I always awoke screaming in terror. It stopped, never to return again, after the birth of our first child, Michael, in 1949. Robin's arrival five years later marked the end of transition and the beginning of my integration. From then on I was at home.

In 1956 a chance opportunity to choreograph the dances for a school production of *The Bartered Bride* opened new doors for me. There were favourable reviews of my work in the press, people read them and became interested, and I was asked to teach some classes of children, teenagers and adults. Invitations to choreograph in theatre and opera followed, and as my love for dance was rekindled, I realised with delight that Belfast was ready and eager to accept and embrace modern dance, a dance form it had not known before. The wealth of talent I found among my pupils led eventually to the foundation of the Belfast Modern Dance Group.

All my early hopes and dreams found expression and realisation through teaching these gifted and highly motivated young people, and through watching their artistic progress. After a long time of stagnation, dance had again become a life force.

Nothing of this would have been possible had I not had Harry's and the boys' total understanding, encouragement and support. Family and Dance lived side by side and finally blended into a life of fulfilment.

Ӎ. Кр

Просьба

можчу

Вог

бодосе

Кр